'The beauty of this book is that whatever stage you are at in your career, I believe the sound advice and case studies (based on extensive coaching and professional experience) are something that everyone can benefit from. The structured framework covers every aspect from the initial "where do I start?" to actually getting on the right path and all the relevant steps in between. The exercises and very practical tips stood out for me as key to personalizing each stage of the journey when *Taking Charge of Your Career*. It's not an easy journey but with Jane and Camilla's help it just got easier!'

Blair Beavis, Early Talent Manager EMEA, Johnson & Johnson

'A fantastic one-stop guide for taking a proactive approach to your own career management. Clear, insightful and practical – these authors know their stuff and it shows. Helpful and motivating in equal measure.'

Susan Gatell, Careers Adviser, Cambridge University

'A thorough, structured and pragmatic overview to career management that covers both the practical aspects of changing careers in our volatile, uncertain world, with the often harder, personal underlying challenges many people have to face and overcome to move forward. The book starts with exploring the underlying psychological issues of fear, risk, limiting beliefs and motivations, before moving on to understanding yourself and what you're looking for, with some excellent tools that are easy to use. The personal brand, networking and research chapters in *Taking Charge of your Career* will help anyone planning a career transition to both prepare and act so they can be their best in career conversations and transitions.'

Stuart Jagot, Director of Career Development at Saïd Business School, University of Oxford

'Finally, a book that connects the mechanics of the job search to the critical motivations that should drive the direction of the search. Only by combining these dimensions can a job seeker hope to achieve genuine job and career fulfilment. Arnold and Barrett provide us the impulse and the practical tools to do just that with great flair.'

Nicolas Constantinesco, former Associate Principal at McKinsey and founder of Promeo

'I have turned to *Taking Charge of Your Career* many times over the years since it was first published – both for those I coach through career change as well as at times for myself. Just about everything you need to think about when considering a career change is included in this gem of a career guide. The new edition is even more packed with straightforward and actionable tools. The section on job hunting, where Jane and Camilla address the importance of demonstrating your fit for a role by connecting emotionally with an interviewer, couldn't be more true! I recommend this book for both career coaching professionals as well as jobseekers everywhere.'

Mary Carey, Regional Director, INSEAD Executive Education; former Global Director, INSEAD Career Development Center

'*Taking Charge of Your Career* has helped me a lot in planning and executing a clear strategy in two of the most difficult aspects of my professional career: finding the right career goal that best fits me, and a plan to achieve it. The book is very well structured, it provides frameworks and exercises that help you in discovering yourself, what you truly want and what you should be looking for. It incorporates examples and case studies to make it comprehensive. I wish I had read this book 10 years ago.'

Yair Marc Martinez Palomino, Consultant at Accenture

'Jane Barrett and Camilla Arnold have together created a comprehensive and encouraging handbook for the motivated career changer, with engaging case studies of successful career changers who have followed their passion.'

Clare Brachi Stott, MBA Career Development Manager, University of Bath School of Management

'This is a practical, straightforward book that details the key stages of managing and changing careers with a really useful mix of advice, exercises and tips brought to life with real life case studies. Both Camilla and Jane have decades of experience in this field, which is so evident in the book.'

Cathy Holley, Partner, Boyden Executive Search

'If you are looking for a practical, detailed and well thought-out career book then look no further. Camilla and Jane have certainly done their homework and provide the answers to the key questions you should be considering.'

Jon Mitchell, Executive Coach and author of *Careers After the Armed Forces: How to decide on the right career and make a successful transition*

'This book takes you systematically through the career transformation process, from self-assessment to successful job hunting. Jane and Camilla's book helps overcome any anxiety, doubt or the agony of making choices in the face of change by providing a solid framework for taking sound career management decisions. Jane and Camilla are well placed for providing this advice: both have worked in recruitment so they have a solid understanding of what makes a candidate stand out and what companies look for in candidates, and have very extensive experience in coaching and career counselling.'

Rosie Innes, Associate Director, Career Management Delivery, IESE Business School

'Feeling stuck in your career? Frustrated by books only covering elements of the job search process, being too theoretical or out of date? *Taking Charge of Your Career* is grounded in the realities of the modern-day job search and gives real-life examples to guide you in implementing the ideas within. Pick up this book today and your successful future self will thank you for it!'

Brian Marrinan, Former Head of Talent Development E&Y and Managing Partner of Journey Partners

'Jane and Camilla are a fantastic source of careers advice and some of my favourite interviewees. In *Taking Charge of Your Career* they combine in-depth knowledge and real breadth of experience with a lightness of touch, which makes the book a pleasure to read.'

Rhymer Rigby, Journalist and author of *The Careerist: Over 100 Ways to Get Ahead at Work*

'This is a great one-stop-shop of information, insight and resources for anyone looking to reinvigorate their career. Many career guides will claim to help you to uncover your skills, values and interests, but too often leave you thinking, "That's great. Now what?" Jane Barrett and Camilla Arnold provide the structured framework to help you to uncover your underlying strengths and interests, but as importantly, the practical steps to help translate those insights into tangible career options.

Pragmatic, accessible and full of helpful exercises, case studies and practical tips, this guide brings together all you need to take charge of your career. I'd highly recommend it!'

Margaret O'Neill, Career Coach, London Business School

'Camilla and Jane's approach has helped me to integrate all aspects of my life to help me to grow in confidence and grow professionally. Their snippets of day-to-day wisdom have been invaluable. They draw on stories and examples which are so easy to remember. I used to think this sort of stuff was common sense but it really isn't – it's a powerful and accessible tool that I am now recommending to everyone!'

Charlie Howard, Founder MAC UK and The Integrate Movement (TIM), Social Entrepreneur and Clinical Psychologist

Taking Charge of Your Career

Taking Charge of Your Career

The Essential Guide to Finding the Job That's Right for You

by Camilla Arnold and Jane Barrett

Bloomsbury Business
An imprint of Bloomsbury Publishing Plc

B L O O M S B U R Y

LONDON · OXFORD · NEW YORK · NEW DELHI · SYDNEY

Bloomsbury Business

An imprint of Bloomsbury Publishing Plc

50 Bedford Square	1385 Broadway
London	New York
WC1B 3DP	NY 10018
UK	USA

www.bloomsbury.com

First published 2017

British Library Cataloguing-in-Publication Data
A catalogue record for this book is available from the British Library.

ISBN:	PB:	978-1-4729-2992-1
	ePDF:	978-1-4729-3336-2
	ePub:	978-1-4729-3335-5

Library of Congress Cataloging-in-Publication Data
Names: Arnold, Camilla, author. | Barrett, Jane, 1971- author.
Title: Taking charge of your career : the essential guide to finding the career that's right for you / by Camilla Arnold and Jane Barrett.
Other titles: If not now, when?
Description: Second edition. | London ; New York, NY : Bloomsbury Business, 2017. | Earlier edition published in 2010 as: If not now, when? : how to take charge of your career | Includes bibliographical references and index.
Identifiers: LCCN 2016035466 (print) | LCCN 2016048579 (ebook) | ISBN 9781472929921 (pbk.) | ISBN 9781472933355 (ePub) | ISBN 9781472933362 (ePDF) | ISBN 9781472933379 (xml)
Subjects: LCSH: Career development. | Career changes. | Success in business.
Classification: LCC HF5381 .A8239495 2017 (print) | LCC HF5381 (ebook) | DDC
650.14--dc23
LC record available at https://lccn.loc.gov/2016035466

Cover design: Liron Gilenberg / ironicitalics.com

Typeset by Fakenham Prepress Solutions, Fakenham, Norfolk NR21 8NN
Printed and bound in Great Britain

Contents

Acknowledgements

Thank you to my mum and dad for their unconditional support over the years and for encouraging me to flourish. And thank you to Michelle Walder who has been the ultimate career catalyst and personal cheerleader. I dedicate the book to Harrison Arnold, Jemima Arnold, Noah Roche and Jude Roche – I hope you each find the career path that brings you joy and fulfilment. Camilla

Thank you to my mother Pip who has always been there for me through the ups and downs and my husband Colin for his unwavering support. I dedicate the book to my son Tom and my niece and nephew, Florence and Jamie Elliott – may this guide you on your own career journey. Jane

Thank you to everyone who has contributed their stories and insights to the book, showing just what is possible with drive, enthusiasm and motivation. Thank you to Akosua Afriyie-Kumi, Adrian Arnold, Colin Barrett, Laura Bevill, Elizabeth Bird, Kate Clifford, Kathryn Davis, Patrick Dudley Smith, Emma Greggains, Jude Hawkins, Carla Holden, Jennifer Hollaway, Kaye Kent, Julia E. Knight, Guy Jeremiah, Jo Lane, Christoph Langwallner, Jamie Lumley, Sarah Marsh, John McFarland, Tina Moran, Amit Pandey, Chris Penny, Tony Restell, Lindsay Small, John Smith, Henry Teare, Robert Timothy, Janie Van Hool, Klaudiusz Zwolinski.

We would also like to thank all our clients over the years who have helped develop this methodology with their successes and their feedback.

Where possible the names in the case studies are real. A few have been changed to protect privacy.

Introduction

We wanted to write a book that *we* would have wanted to read when each of us was going through our own career reviews and then later as career coaches; a book we would want to use to support our clients. It's true that there are many career books on the market but we felt there were none that cover the whole process from deciding what you have to offer and what you want, right through to the practicalities of securing the work you want to do, with real life case studies to encourage you along the way. Most people don't have the time or inclination to read several books on this important topic – so we decided to put everything in one place and look at all the main areas that our clients ask us to cover with them.

This book is based on over thirty years' experience of managing careers, both our own and those of the clients we have worked with. It also draws on our experience of recruitment, both in-house and for executive recruitment companies, as well as working in the field of career development with many different people, from graduates and non-graduates to executives ranging from journalists to venture capitalists. We have created a book that reflects everything we have learnt and sets out a clear, simple structure with tips and techniques to help you analyse and plan the next step of your career. Throughout the book there are examples of people who have successfully found work that is satisfying, meaningful and 'fits' them. Career management is not an exact science and consequently many people haven't a clue where to start – a feeling in the past we have known only too well! In our experience many people who are unhappy in their current role, or unsure how to develop their career; want to take control rather than let their career 'happen' but they're just not sure how to get started.

It's up to you

What we do to earn money takes up a huge proportion of our time and affects many areas of our life, so it makes sense to devote time and energy to actively working on it and to make it as enjoyable as possible. Having said that, most people will spend more time and effort deciding on their next holiday, gadget or clothes purchase! Over the past twenty-five years, career management has changed immeasurably. Once it was the responsibility of the company you joined straight from school or university to guide your career as you progressed up the totem pole, with employees rarely changing career or even company. Today, it is falling to the individual to manage their career, deciding where they want to go, how to get there and which organization or part of an organization would be the best place to get that experience.

As a career can have such a huge impact on both everyday and long-term happiness, we encourage you to do everything you can to ensure you are in the right place, doing something that aligns with what you value and helps you progress to your ultimate goal. For many of us the right field of work in our twenties might not reflect the person we are later on in our lives. Sometimes a review is enforced by redundancy or you may find yourself wanting to change aspects of your career as your life circumstances change. This book will help you consider your choices so you have a personal framework to analyse your career options.

Reality check

One caveat at this point: many people say that they'll know they have found the right career for them if they bounce out of bed in the morning, eager to get to work. The reality is that if you find your perfect job, this may not happen every day. We will aim to keep your feet on the ground as you work your way through the book, but we have seen so many people find the right career at the right time for them, that we believe you can do the same.

It can take time to move towards a job you'll love and time to structure your work to better suit who you are, but the rewards, if you stick with it, are immeasurable. Your career also needs regular review (ideally annually) as you or your circumstances change. By structuring your thinking using the exercises in this book, you can save time and gain more satisfaction from working towards your goal. It is apparent that in either boom or bust, no one manages your career better than you, as only you know what is right for you. It makes sense that people increasingly want to manage their career more proactively to get the best return for the money spent on education and the many hours they put in at work, not just leaving it to chance. That is where this book comes in.

Why did we write this book?

Through our workshops and one-to-one work, we have coached thousands of people through this methodology to find successful, fulfilling careers and new roles. We have also both changed our own careers, so know first hand the anxieties, obstacles and finally relief and pleasure at finding the right career path both in the short and long term.

Case study: Jane

Originally I trained as a chartered surveyor, having been advised by my school career adviser to do a more vocational degree than geography, my best subject. I found I was interested more in people than buildings and embarked on a quest to work out what I really wanted to do. This was more difficult than I imagined. The government-run guidance offices didn't seem to offer much advice on finding work that suited me, and my university careers centre was more geared towards recent students graduating. After my surveying exams I moved to a recruitment firm, thinking naively it was all about 'helping people find work'. Blinded by the money (my values around this time were very money-orientated as I had student loans to pay back!) I joined the IT recruitment division. With too much emphasis on sales, after two years I moved up the value chain and joined a headhunting company. With a less overt sales culture, I found more satisfaction in delivering a more professional service; but I found I enjoyed the candidate-facing work the most, which was not what I was being paid to do!

At this point I was unfulfilled. Having made some career mistakes in the past (or that was how I saw them) I was reluctant to make a change and was stuck in inertia. On holiday I read an article on career coaching and on my return hired a coach to help me work out my next step. She used insightful questioning to help me discover what was important to me, what I had to offer and what motivated me.

Then I began the path to setting up my own career coaching and information company. I made a gradual transition, easing into this with some part-time recruitment contracts to allow me to gain more knowledge about what employers were looking for and give me time to retrain as a career coach. I started to build relationships with business schools who could give me a steady stream of clients to support my practice. The business has evolved into its current format and delivers career coaching and information via webinars, workshops and online training to leading business schools worldwide.

There have been some blind alleys on the way, including setting up an eco products business (environment is a strong value for me). This ultimately failed as I was too late to the market and I wasn't prepared to invest the time and money required. It was a false start but one from which I learned so much. I have now developed this interest within Career Farm through a programme of specialist webinars helping people get into sustainability and impact investing careers.

The path I have taken to get where I am now has not been smooth. There have been many ups and downs. Like many of my clients I have had to reassess and pivot as my needs and circumstances have changed. The world of work changes rapidly and if you are not actively managing your career you can feel out of control and at the mercy of circumstances. I hope the process in this book is something people can come back to as they navigate their career and use the structure to analyse and make plans to develop their career.

Case study: Camilla

My career started like that of most of my friends and early colleagues. We fell into jobs that seemed to be as good as any other at the time and had some scope for progression. It was a rarity to come across someone who absolutely knew what they wanted to do and had made choices from A levels and university onwards towards that goal. To be honest, I looked at these strange creatures with a mixture of awe and envy, wondering why I couldn't work out what was the right direction for me.

The perennial advice then, as now, was to work out what you were interested in and then find a career from that and the options offered by my school career's advisor didn't deviate from the tried and tested fields of teacher, nurse or PA. The only problem with that was that I really didn't think that there was anything in particular that interested me enough to put all my 'eggs in that basket'. Socializing and travel didn't really seem to offer many long-term career options that appealed. I have been hugely fortunate in the different jobs I have done. I have enjoyed each and every one and learned from them all. I always felt like I was moving forward. The only problem was that it just felt like a series of jobs that I fell into through referral or happy circumstance rather than a career per se.

Each time I thought I was ready for a new direction, I would buy the latest book on how to identify your passion and find that I was still fairly clueless as to what the next steps would be. Instead, I listened to what other colleagues and friends said were my strengths and orientated my career around that – namely my ability to organize effectively and problem solve. As a result I had an eclectic career based upon those perceived strengths, ever hopeful I would stumble across the perfect job for me, but I don't think I ever quite believed it would happen.

After twenty years of working, I finally did exactly that – I stumbled across coaching (a form of problem solving) and the concept of a portfolio career, which would allow me to have the variety that I loved. I spent three years transitioning from my previous role as

Operations Director for a leading headhunting firm to my current career and I finally feel I have found the right road for me. It would not suit everyone but it harnesses all my strengths, my preferences for working environment and rewards, while still offering new challenges as I constantly refine my career path as I develop and identify new aspirations.

At each stage of this career transition, I have revised and reviewed where I am and whether it works for me. I tried coaching full-time and found I missed the buzz of the office and interaction with colleagues, so I re-evaluated and after much searching, joined a company focused on coaching and leadership development – TXG Ltd – whose values and drive to be the best in the business matched mine exactly. I am now Managing Director, Client Services and advise blue chip corporate clients on executive coaching and leadership development initiatives while acting as a broker for the best coaching talent worldwide. I also continue to coach private individuals who are at a career crossroads. This allows me the flexibility I was searching for and allows me to express all aspects of who I am in the work place. I coach a wide range of clients from CEOs, board directors and career professionals who are looking to work to their best potential through to those seeking their perfect career and not sure where to start, ranging from recent graduates to retirees.

For both of us looking back, if we had known then what we know now (how many times do people say that?!) we both agree we could probably have shortened the whole process and had a clearer idea of where we were going. Our journeys from job to chosen career have been long ones. We spent years searching for the right careers and we became frustrated at the lack of informed practical advice to get moving. The books we read tended to skim over the top of the subject and while we ended up with a glut of information, there was little practical advice on how then to decide on a career option. Advice from well-intentioned advisors was that if you had a good job, why rock the boat? That is why we work with clients looking for help as they search for a new role and why we decided to write this book. Sadly there is no crystal ball and we can't tell you what the perfect career is for you.

However what we can do is share the process in this book which we have found is the best way to help our clients find their own way – as, in the long run, you deciding your own career path is much more satisfying and much more likely to work than us or anyone else telling you what to do. After all, no one can know you as well as you know yourself. We hope that it provides you with a structure, based on years of experience, that is clear, easy to follow, pragmatic and takes you beyond a download of information to how to follow through to your ultimate goal of a great career that you manage proactively. We truly believe it is possible for anyone to do the same if they have the motivation and drive to keep going, even when the going gets tough. It should also be a fun exploration of you and your personal brand.

What this book will give you

- A structured series of exercises which focus on each specific element of career review and planning
- Clarity about what is <u>really</u> important to you in your working life and what is 'nice to have'
- Insights from the stories of other people who have been through a career change and successfully come out the other side

- A reference book you can return to again and again throughout your career that covers the key aspects of career planning and change
- A proven system that works. We keep in touch with our clients to ensure these exercises and advice is still helpful and relevant across sectors, industries and geographies
- A way to investigate career options in a logical and structured way
- An action plan and timetable to move forward, backed up by solid analysis

Often people start thinking about their career when a crisis hits: they have been made redundant, had a low salary review or have been passed over for promotion. In an ideal world, this kind of outside influence should not be the catalyst to thinking about your career, as the emotion attached to this can cloud your thinking and then a new job search starts from a position of hurt, anger and resentment rather than enthusiasm, drive and commitment. For many people looking to change their job, the focus is often on the 'I need to get a job now' issues (CVs, job search strategy, getting interviews etc.) in parallel with the longer-term 'I want to find a job that fits me better'.

Career choices can seem confusing and overwhelming at times but it can be reassuring to work through a proven process in order to analyse your career. Once you have completed the book, you will have a much better understanding of what you want and what you have to offer. The career framework you will have created by the end of the book will be a summary of your personal data collected in a methodical way. This will help you to make an informed choice, minimizing the chance you will make the wrong decision.

How to use the book

Our experience has shown that what you get out of the process and the clarity you have at the end of the process depends entirely on how much you put into it. It can be tempting just to read through a book like this, vowing to get back to the exercises at a later date. Unfortunately this approach is not going to lead to any lasting changes. We strongly encourage you to complete all the exercises as you come across them. If you would like soft copies of the exercises, you will find them at the website www.howto-takechargeofyourcareer.com along with other resources that may be useful. Keep an action planning sheet so you create momentum and a time line for completing the various tasks, all of which we'll cover later. You will then start to reap the rewards of your hard work.

Many people will be able to complete the exercises and will have a support team and the motivation to set them on the path to proactively managing their career. However, some may find this more challenging and wish to partner with a friend who is also embarking on a career search or work with a career coach. There are many career coaches in the market – some good, some not so good. Later in the book, we will give you some insider knowledge of how to choose the right one for you.

Who is this book for?

Whether you are looking for a new job or seeking a promotion, planning to change career or set up your own business, this book has been written for you so that you get the most satisfaction out of your work.

Our experience has shown that the knowledge you will gain in the book will give you an advantage if you are:

Looking for a new job – as a candidate, if you know what you want and what you can offer, you will be more compelling as a potential employee than those who haven't worked that out.

Looking to be promoted or progress within an organization – if you know clearly what skills you have, what you want to develop and where you are heading in terms of your career, you are far more likely to achieve your goals.

Finding the right career direction – if you are clear about what you are looking for, what skills you bring and you have done the research to confirm your career choice, you will have a clear direction when starting your job search.

Setting up a new business – ensuring that setting up a business serves your personal needs, values and skills is the key to success and may also help you when you hire staff to complement your skills.

Post-retirement – analysing your working life to date, the skills you have accumulated and your preferences will help in finding a role to suit you if you decide to keep working in a voluntary or part-time role.

Embarking upon education – if you have identified your long-term aims for your career, you are more likely to make sure you are on the right course and, once you are on that course, ensure you maximize the opportunities that this provides.

In summary

Many of the articles and books that have been written on the subject will target only one particular aspect of the search for the ideal career – whether it is identifying your passion, understanding portfolio working, creating the perfect CV or answering the most dastardly of interview questions. Many of these books may be useful to you and we recommend the best in the 'Resources' section at the back of the book. By covering all the key aspects of a career search and ongoing career planning in one book, we believe you can complete the fundamental groundwork to really know yourself, what you are looking for and understand all the steps to get there. There are no guarantees in life but our tried and tested methodology will lead you to making an informed decision, based on skill identification and research, to create an action plan to get you where you want to go.

If there is a particular stage that you are tempted to miss out, it is probably the stage that will hold the key to the direction for you to take. We will encourage you to network (which usually makes people's spirits falter at the mere mention of the word) but we will also give you tips about how to make the process as painless as possible. Sadly there is no getting around networking – it has huge value not only in identifying your next career or the next role but also in developing your long-term career. It is easy to sit back and just go with the flow, avoiding the more difficult aspects of striving for a great career. Rather than just allowing life to happen to you, we encourage you to become proactive because the rewards really are worth it.

We all have choices in life but if you have ever contemplated a career change, or tried to identify a career path that excites you, we ask the question: if not now, when?

Part I: If not now, when? What is holding you back?

Choose a job you love, and you will never have to work a day in your life.

Confucius

Dealing with obstacles may seem an unusual place to start in a book about seizing the moment and making a change in your career – yet when we speak to people for the first time, often the first thing they want to talk about is all the problems that might get in the way of their success.

Those areas of concern include:

- lack of motivation
- limiting beliefs about their ability to find something that works for them
- frustration and anger if a career change has been forced on them (i.e. through redundancy, illness or other life-changing circumstance)
- lack of time
- lack of money or unwillingness to take a drop in salary or retrain
- family and/or friends questioning why they are considering a change.

We have covered each of these areas of concern below to give you some ideas of how you might overcome them and how others who have faced similar concerns have found a way to move forward. If you find that any of these, or indeed other concerns, are slowing you down or stopping you from realizing your potential, you may want to consider finding some professional help to deal with those issues once and for all.

Chapter 1

Overcoming fear and risk

No one can cheat you out of ultimate success but yourself.
Ralph Waldo Emerson

Fear can be paralyzing, but knowing and understanding what your fear is can be the first step to facing it. The best antidote to fear when going through a career change is to work out whether your fear is based in reality or is merely a perception. So, it is reality that you can't become a brain surgeon without having trained as a doctor, but it is a perception that they don't accept people over twenty-five on to courses to train as doctors. By naming the fear, you can then gather evidence to ascertain what is real and what is assumed and dismiss the negative perceptions that are holding you back. Many people seem to feel that if they do nothing, it will all work out eventually and they will deal with bumps in the road as they come along. They will do almost anything not to make a choice to move forward. The irony is that deciding to do nothing is also a choice and often means that they are at the whim of factors outside their control.

Calculated risk

There's no getting around it: at some point, if you are going to move forward, you will have to take a leap of faith, but by basing it on research and knowledge, it *will* feel less daunting. There's a moment in *Indiana Jones and the Last Crusade* when Indiana is faced with a seemingly insurmountable chasm to cross to get to the Holy Grail. He knows his subject and his journey to that point has been reliant on his knowledge to avoid the pitfalls put in his way. At the chasm, he has to trust what he knows and the research that has been done and steps out into the seeming abyss to find a hidden bridge. What would it take for you to take that leap of faith in your search for your career?

If you are getting stuck, it can be useful to highlight the sticking points and come up with an action plan to solve them.

PROBLEM/STICKING POINT	RESOLUTION OPTIONS
e.g.	e.g.
I won't make enough money for at least two years to support my current lifestyle	Review current lifestyle and see where there are potential savings I could sustain for two years
	Build up a savings account to cover the difference between the new salary and the amount needed to support my lifestyle
	Take out a professional and career development loan for the retraining and use savings for extra living expenses over the next two years

Chapter 2

Finding the right motivation and attitude

Necessity is the mother of invention.

Proverb

If there is one thing that we have found over and over again as we work with people going through the process of deciding on a career direction or career change, it's that the ones who are successful are motivated and have the right positive attitude. The people who get to the end of the exercises and research knowing their future career direction are the ones who have soldiered on past obstacles, scepticism, nerves, lack of confidence and time constraints. We know from experience that this is often easier said than done, but we hope this section will help you when you come across some of the hurdles that will surely occur as you work your way through the book.

Finding your motivation

It is so important you find the motivation within yourself to make the change. Just flicking through this book hoping that change will happen by osmosis is sadly not going to work, as only you can put in the work to make it happen. It also rarely works well if you are pushing someone to make a career change, working your way through the book on their behalf (perhaps you're a well-meaning parent or partner).

Once you have found your motivation, it's important to find and maintain your positive attitude, even when the chips are down. We hope we can help you achieve that attitude by providing case studies of people who have been down this road before you and been successful. Sometimes when you are struggling, this means having to 'fake it till you make it' – faking the confidence and self-belief until things start to fall into place. It is surprising how effective that can be as a strategy to keep the momentum going and move through your doubts. There has been plenty of research and even television shows that have taken people out of their comfort zone and taught them how to fake a situation until they have achieved the insider language, the confidence and the basic skills to make people believe in them and their abilities. The faking can be tough to start off with, whether it is convincing people you are confident and positive about the career you have decided upon or overcoming nerves to go along to an information gathering interview. We have seen time and time again that there is a point where you move from being a faker to the person who has made it and it starts to become second nature. You can use the same strategies as we go through this methodology together and it is amazing how effective it can be, especially if you are feeling a little sceptical or lacking in confidence. Once you have some experience – even if it is unpaid or for a relatively short period of time – it can often be 'enough' to help you to come across as knowledgeable in that area.

As a relatively new consultant following his career change, James was only ever asked about what he could do for his clients and what examples he had of recent successes. They never asked how long he had been consulting, which definitely helped when he was starting out. James had learnt to be confident in a new area where he had limited experience, although what little he did have was extremely relevant. He never volunteered the information about how little experience he had and he chose to focus on what he could do.

All change is risky and, as human beings, many of us will do almost anything to avoid change until we have no alternative. While you can't remove all the risk when it comes to progressing or changing your career, sometimes staying where you are may actually be the more risky option and much less satisfying in the long term. For some, it can take years to transition to a new career, retrain or progress within an organization, so it can be a gradual process where you can test the water rather than having to commit too much too soon.

Attitude to change exercise

If you do find your resolve wobbling and worry that perhaps this is just all too much trouble, it's worth considering the following questions:

If I do nothing at all, where might I be in five years' time?

....

How do you feel about this answer?

....

What is the risk to you of not making a change?

....

What is the block that is getting in your way?

....

If that block was no longer an issue, what would you do next?

....

We encourage you to keep going even if you realize that your career change or progression is going to take longer than you envisaged. The end result will be worth it and you are not alone – many career changers have faced the same concern but were so pleased that they kept going. You may also find that once you have decided on your career move, you get blown off course by an unexpected event or change in circumstances; however, if you keep the momentum, drive and attitude, and if you know where you are heading, then you are much more likely to reach your destination.

Case study: Henry Teare

Having gone to university and done a business degree, I still wasn't sure what I wanted to do for a career. A lot of friends were going into banking and I thought I should do the same, as it seemed like a good idea to pay off some debts. I soon realized that I didn't want to be a small cog in a large machine and fell into selling advertising space for a small firm instead. Still unfulfilled, I finally realized, having always known it deep down, that I dreamed of doing something creative with my hands, away from an office environment.

Disappointed with the haircuts I had been getting, I started cutting my own hair and then friends started asking to have theirs done too. At that stage, I was looking at getting into carpentry, landscape gardening or building and hadn't really thought about hairdressing as an option. Then one night I awoke in a panic, worried about a presentation to a media agency I hadn't really prepared for, and it clicked. I couldn't carry on like this. I had to be happy, passionate and proud of my work. I started thinking about which profession was going to suit me the most and the more I thought about hairdressing, the more it ticked the right lifestyle choices. I'd be creative and active in my work, gain a skill with the potential to travel and, most importantly, make people happy every day. I set about meeting hairdressers and getting work experience evenings and weekends. The more I did it, the more I wanted to learn. Then I met a former Vidal Sassoon Educator who was setting up a salon and I jumped at the opportunity to join him. I knew it was going to be tough financially and that I had to train from the bottom again, but I had to give it a go. It took a couple of years of hard work but once I realized I was an able hairdresser, I finally became proud of my achievements for the first time since I was a teenager. I am now five years into my hairdressing career and recently got a job at a top salon, James Brown, in the West End of London. Those early days of worrying about failing are all in the past and I am looking forward to opening new doors in hairdressing.

What helped me initially was to imagine myself in the same job in five to ten years' time. Did I want to be that person? Unhappy in my work and unfulfilled, stuck in a rut? I think the key is to be passionate, whether it's about a skill, service or product you sell, then take small steps towards finding out more about it. The learning will then come easily. That passion will drive success and a better quality of life will follow.

Chapter 3

Limiting beliefs

Insanity is doing the same thing in the same way and expecting a different outcome.

Chinese proverb

One thing is certain as you go through this process. You will face obstacles along the way, both real and imagined, and whether you get past them or get stuck comes down largely to attitude.

Often the most powerful hurdles we face are the imagined ones. If you have ever had coaching or read anything about the subject, you may have heard these described as self-limiting beliefs. These are the beliefs that we have gathered through life that may, at some time, have worked well for us but we rarely examine whether they are still helpful. These beliefs often start from things we hear from an early age – common examples are things like:

'I have never been very bright'

'It's a pipe dream to expect to find the perfect job'

'My family have always struggled in the workplace and I expect the same will be true for me'

'My dad always joked with me that I had great plans but never achieved them'

'I'm lucky to have a job – thinking I can find something I'll enjoy as I earn money is not reality'

'I am never going to be a big earner'

'I tend to drift and be a bit lazy – my teacher used to tell me that I was never going to get to the highest levels of a career'

'I was told by my professor that I should stick to working with figures as I wasn't that great with people'

The list could go on and on. So the first step for you at this stage is to be honest with yourself and write a list of the thoughts that are getting in your way. Do you think you'll fail? Why? The more things you uncover, the better!

Camilla coached someone who had been put off becoming a copywriter when she was fifteen after her grandmother and farmer father had said that it didn't sound a good way to earn a living. When we discussed what they were basing that belief on, she discussed it with both of them and they couldn't remember the conversation that had stopped her career dream in its tracks. She went on to study copywriting part-time, took the time to talk to people in the field before making the move into advertising full-time. It may seem obvious, but you always have a choice over how you react to what is said to you. It is up to you how you hear what is being said. When someone offers advice or points you away from a direction you are thinking about, it is always worth asking yourself why they have given you that advice, what they have based it on and whether they see your future in the same way as you do. You can then decide to take that advice or not, or just chalk it up as an opinion that is not helpful in this instance. Our experience is that those who find the career path that feels 'right' often spend their time with people who have achieved what they set out to achieve. They get the most supportive comments from them as they know anything is possible. They have been there, done that and got the t-shirt!

Identifying obstacles exercise

Getting to the bottom of your limiting beliefs is really important, so that you recognize them should they start getting in your way and hopefully will be able to deal with them one at a time. You will find, as we continue, that more of these limiting beliefs pop up either in your own head or contributed by well-meaning friends and family. Keep going back to this first action step to validate whether it is something to bear in mind or to leave to one side and move on.

1   List one self-limiting belief.

    ....

2   Who told you this?

    ....

3   Is their opinion based on fact or evidence or is it their opinion? If you are not sure, ask them to give you some evidence to back up what they're saying.

    ....

4   Are they equipped to give you good advice on the particular subject they are commenting on?

    ....

5   Do you know someone else you can check this advice or statement with?

    ....

As you keep adding to your list of self-limiting beliefs, ask yourself if it is helping or hindering you? If you were to suspend that belief for a moment, how differently would you approach the situation? Sometimes these worries come from within. Perhaps you have had a bad day and wonder: Am I clever enough? Or: I don't interview well so what's the point? Or: I'll never be able to do that so I may as well not try. There are those self-limiting beliefs again. You will find that this is a bit like peeling an onion – just when you think you've got to the last layer, there's another one, but the more you uncover and deal with, the fewer obstacles you are likely to face!

Jane remembers telephoning one of her oldest friends to tell her that she was moving from recruitment to be a career coach. The friend shouted to her husband while on the phone to her, saying: 'Jane says she's going to be a career coach! You can't make any money doing that can you?' then she categorically told her they thought she would never make any money from career coaching. Several years passed and Jane set up a successful career coaching business. Ironically Jane stayed over one night with these friends before she delivered a career coaching workshop at a local university, which incidentally she got paid for!

When you are dealing with your limiting beliefs, it can be difficult to stay positive because for so many of us, the doubts and negative thoughts seem to flow so much easier. If that resonates with you, then perhaps it is worth creating a 'positives' folder. This folder can be filled with any positive feedback you have received over the years: cards, letters of recommendation, good reports, thank you emails from managers or colleagues – you get the idea. When you start to wonder whether you have the ability, reading through some of those can help get you back to reality and provide solid evidence of your abilities. This file can also come in useful when you are compiling a CV to remind you of your achievements or skills.

It can also be helpful to enlist the support of a friend or perhaps a family member who will challenge some of your thinking at times. One word of warning: choose people who are supportive and challenging rather than those who are well-intentioned but seem to have an agenda of their own (i.e. does it suit them if you stay at the same level as them? Do they see you in a certain way and not want you to change? etc.).

Chapter 4

The power of choice

> The greatest weapon against stress is our ability to choose one thought over another.
>
> *William James*

Choice can be a wonderful thing – it gives us a sense of control and power over our lives and when we embrace it, it can set us on the path to unlocking our potential. Choice can also be daunting and something that we regularly try and avoid by prevarication and hesitation. We forget that prevarication and hesitation are also choices. So our question to you is: Are you ready to choose optimism? Are you ready to choose to move forward? Are you ready to choose a road that may be strewn with difficulties but that ultimately can lead you to the career of your dreams? No? Perhaps your circumstances are such that now isn't the right time and that's OK. There are short and long paths to finding the career that you are seeking and your circumstances may well affect which path you opt for. We just urge you to be mindful of the choices you are making and what you are doing or not doing to contribute to your end goal, each and every day. However, if you have chosen to pick up this book rather than shrug your shoulders and walk past the section on careers, you have made a positive start! So often the journey can feel like it is full of obstacles but the realization that you have ultimate choice on how to view or indeed tackle those obstacles can give you back your sense of power.

So first things first:

- What choice are you going to make?
- Are you ready to start looking at your career right now? Or does it feel like this is not the right time?
- Are you willing to commit to spending fifteen minutes a day to discover more about yourself to start building a picture of the right career path for you? Or are you swamped with work, tired with a new baby, or just not feeling motivated?
- Are you willing to push yourself beyond your comfort zone to ask for help or to reach out to someone you've never met? Or would you prefer to do your research at this stage on the internet and staying 'hidden'?
- Are you looking for opportunities around you every day to build your skill set, understand your transferable skills or ask for feedback on how you can improve? Or would you rather think about this some more before you let people know what you are planning?

And so the list goes on. All of the above questions have legitimate answers and only you can know whether you are ready to really commit to moving forward towards your ideal career. The choice is always yours – to keep going or stop, to start or prevaricate, but each one of them is your choice.

What is yours going to be?

Chapter 5

I didn't choose to make a change – it's been forced on me

When it is dark enough, you can see the stars.

Ralph Waldo Emerson

Sometimes we face life-changing events that can throw us off course, even if that course wasn't right for us anyway. How you respond after you have dealt with the immediate aftermath of any life-changing event, where something happens that is outside your control, often determines whether you are able to move forward in a constructive way. We have seen at first hand how hard this can be and we know there will be ups and downs, but we have also seen that it is increasingly common for a life-changing event to send people in a new or more focused direction.

Case study: John Smith

I spent twenty years in the investment banking industry, first as an equity market analyst and latterly as a leader of various City firms. My final role was as Global Head of Equities at ABN Amro, with responsibility for 2,500 people in forty-five countries and over €1bn of revenues. I spent my time flying around the world, building teams, deciding strategy, and driving the business to an improved P&L. The change for me came when our third child was diagnosed as autistic just before his fourth birthday. At that stage, Fraser was non-verbal, very difficult behaviourally and a real handful. It was a fairly simple decision to give up work, train as a behavioural therapist and to work full-time with my son. He began to improve, and years later – while still noticeably autistic – he now has lots of language, is a happy and cheerful young man, and we live a relatively normal life.

What was unexpected was how relevant the behavioural work was to my previous world in the City, most particularly around how people learn, what motivates them, and how the behaviour of leaders can influence those that follow them. By this stage, I was also being asked to mentor younger people coming through the ranks in my old industry and it seemed an obvious step to find an outlet for this and to couple it with my behavioural work. As Fraser had begun to improve, I had capacity to do other things, but I still needed flexibility around his needs and deficits. The answer lay in executive coaching. For the past ten years I have built my own coaching practice and have worked with hundreds of clients on a one-on-one basis to help them improve their performance. I have worked in consultancy, accountancy, the legal profession, government, real estate, private equity and multiple investment banks. I now work on average three days a week, have flexibility around when I do this and am lucky enough to have a fulfilling, varied and interesting job. The fulfilment for me comes from seeing people clear obstacles and achieve their potential. For me, the lesson from this was to decide what was important in my life and build work around that rather than the opposite. Coupled with treating a huge challenge as a learning opportunity, I am both delighted and relieved how it has worked out for us all.

Elisabeth Kübler-Ross first introduced her model of the stages of grief in her book *On Death and Dying* (1969). Originally this model was used to understand the stages one might go through when facing a terminal illness, but was later extended to cover other severe personal losses such as a job loss or major change. It's still a useful model for those clients who get stuck at a certain stage so they can see where they are and understand it is a perfectly normal response that they will work their way through.

Stage 1 – Denial
- 'I am not at risk, this isn't happening to me', 'I am too good for this to happen to me'

Stage 2 – Anger
- 'How dare they make me redundant?', 'After all the years of service, this is how they treat me'

Stage 3 – Bargaining
- 'Perhaps if I reduce my hours', 'What if I offer to reduce my pay?'

Stage 4 – Depression
- 'I am on the scrap heap', 'I'll never get another job as good as this'

Stage 5 – Acceptance
- 'It is up to me, so I might as well get on with it', 'Well I might as well look on the bright side'

If you have picked up this book as a result of a life-changing event but are struggling with how to move forward, you might want to consider working with a therapist or coach to help you establish what is getting in your way, whether you are ready to start moving forward and how you are going to do that. As we said at the beginning of this section, as with so many things in life, it is about choice, feeling a positive attitude and if and how you decide to go forward.

Chapter 6

Finding the time and momentum to make it happen

> Do the difficult things while they are easy and do the great things while they are small. A journey of a thousand miles must begin with a single step.
>
> *Lao Tzu*

One of the main perceived obstacles to working on your career can be lack of time. With so many demands on our time, it can feel a very real obstacle, but our experience has shown that, with some small adjustments, it is possible to find the amount of time you'll need to move forward.

If you do think this will be a problem though, it is worth asking yourself if you are sufficiently excited about your goals to commit the time to working towards them. Is there anything you can do to motivate yourself? Can you break down your career change or shift to smaller distinct goals so it feels more manageable? Our experience is that if you set yourself achievable goals that fire you up, you are more likely to prioritize your time and when you analyse how you spend your days, perhaps you can see how you can carve out that little bit of extra time. Perhaps it means watching less TV or getting up half an hour earlier. If you are sufficiently motivated, it will be easier to find creative ways to make time to work on your career. It may mean carving out five minutes each day to do a little more research on the sector you are interested in or to send a couple of emails asking for information. Little and often is potentially as effective as the occasional full day. It is about deciding what works best for you.

While this is not a book on time management (and we recommend one in the References section if you are struggling with the subject), being effective with the time you have to devote to your career will pay dividends. Having a realistic time frame to change career is also important, as many of our clients seem to lose their enthusiasm and momentum if they let the whole process drift. Set yourself goals for each week and month and try and stick to the time frames you have set so you can feel that you are making progress, even if it is one small step at a time. You may want to work with a friend or partner who is also interested in doing a career review to keep each other going throughout the process when one of you starts to flag.

Chapter 7

The money question

> A good decision is based on knowledge and not on numbers.
>
> *Plato*

Money ... possibly the biggest of potential obstacles that holds people back from really going after what they want in their career. Common worries include: Will I have to take a salary cut to retrain? How will I adapt to a reduced cash flow? How will I cope with the financial uncertainty? There is no getting around this subject for most people and it really can't be ignored in the hope it will go away (a technique we have seen many people try over the years!). It is important that you look at the issue, research your options and make a plan so you feel as secure as you can be at every step.

We often liken career changing to deciding to train as a trapeze artist. Career changers often approach the whole thing with a sense of slight excitement but also often an element of fear that they will fail or it won't be possible. They imagine showing up at the big top to learn how to become a trapeze artist and being asked immediately to don the lycra, climb 30 feet in the air, swing on the trapeze and leap as the dashing young man comes swinging towards them with arms outstretched. They seem to feel the same way about approaching a career change – all a bit scary, exhilarating if it works and downright painful if it all goes wrong. No wonder they are daunted. In actuality, the trainer at the big top is there to help you through the learning process with as little pain as possible and preferably without the lycra! You would be fitted with a tight safety harness to keep you safe, and you would start swinging on the trapeze only a few feet above the ground over a safety net. When you are looking to make a change in your career, the first thing to do is define your safety net and safety harness: very often it is money and having a financial cushion to give a sense of protection and safety. Once the safety net and harness are in place, there is a point in this process when you will want to climb higher, take off the safety harness and feel so comfortable on the first trapeze that you are ready to take the leap of faith and be caught by the person on the other trapeze. So, in this analogy – what would your safety harness and safety net look like? Would having enough money to make the change be one of them?'

As you go through the book, there will be a point when you have an idea of what you want to do and an action plan of how you are going to achieve it; then the money hurdle may well appear. It may cost you money, either lost income in terms of a change in salary or the necessity to pay for training, etc. But before you worry that the money hurdle is going to stop you in your tracks, here are just a few things you might want to consider:

- Get real and work out what money you are going to need in your financial safety net or piggy bank to make this happen.
- Devise a specific action plan on how you are going to make that happen.
- Draw up a budget of your monthly expenditure – going through each item to see if there is any room for saving and cutting back.
- Are you going to take a period of time to start saving for the financial safety net?
- Are you going to see if there is a loan available?

- Might you be able to work part-time while you retrain?
- Check again – how much money are you really going to need for a finite amount of time while you make the move and how long can you survive on reduced means?

If money is an issue for you, only you know how much you are going to need to make this happen and reduce your stress. Be realistic. If it takes you a little longer to achieve your goal while you create your financial safety net, it is time well spent so long as you maintain your momentum and find things to do in parallel that advance your career aspirations with further networking, research, etc. Be aware that some careers will require you to find money for retraining and equipment and this obviously needs to be factored into your overall plan. Sometimes it is surprising just how much facilities or equipment cost; this is something to find out in the research phase of your career process. Undoubtedly there are some commitments that are absolutely key (child support payments, mortgage or rent) but even seemingly immoveable commitments might not be as immoveable as you think: we have had clients who have taken their children out of private schools to move to an area where there are good state schools and some who have downsized to a smaller property or relocated to another part of the country where the properties are more affordable in order to release some money to enable a change of career to take place.

Case study: Colin Barrett

In October 1993 I graduated from university with a 2:1 in Philosophy and no idea about what to do with my life. I'd dipped my toe in the water of the university careers centre without much success (apparently only the Roman Catholic Church was interested in employing philosophy graduates), so I started replying to pretty much any advert for a 'graduate' job that appeared in the press. My first job was with a large life assurance company in Kent. From there I moved to Lloyd's of London, and then onto Reuters. There was no great plan, just a desire to be in London and work for a household name. I fell into a job called product management, which involves a small amount of technical knowledge, large amounts of common sense and an ability to be vaguely organized. I did my time in the big corporate, travelled a bit, went out a lot and generally had a good time. However, towards the end of the nineties it became pretty clear to me that I wasn't on anyone's radar to be fast-tracked through the ranks. I worked in a huge sprawling company with a comparatively flat management structure. I got paid well, was competent at my job, but my heart wasn't really in it, and for that reason I think there were a lot of people ahead of me in the queue to move into the heady world of middle management.

About this time I also started to look around at contemporaries who were ten to fifteen years older than me. These people were relatively well paid and in their early to mid-forties and most were deeply cynical about 'work'. As a group they seemed to share two things in common: their company pensions were the main reason they stayed in the job, and they were all petrified of being made redundant at the next internal reorganization (at one point almost a fortnightly event at Reuters). I made two important decisions: 1) no one was going to pluck me from obscurity and mentor me through the ranks and 2) I never ever wanted to be in a position where I wasn't confident about being in charge of my own destiny. For me the change needed to be radical. I knew I had to start again completely. It wasn't easy to acknowledge to myself that the first decade of my working life had been pretty much a waste of time. I had friends who were doing well and advancing professionally, and here was I about to go back to square one. To do this I knew I needed to leave London, and I knew I had to find something which was going to tick all the boxes for me.

Fortunately I was (and still am) lucky enough to be married to an amazing career coach who patiently helped me to identify that role. When all the plans had finally been laid, we moved out of London to Yorkshire, and I started to train for my new career as a financial planner. One of the things I realized very early on was that this was going to be a major financial undertaking. Unless we could bankroll ourselves for at least eighteen months there would just be too much financial pressure and I'd probably end up going back to a product management job based up north. We needed to buy ourselves time, and that involved setting aside a large amount of money. We did this by selling our house in London and instead of trading up, bought an equivalent-sized house in Yorkshire. The price difference allowed us to bank enough money to support us during the early years of my career change.

I started my financial services career right at the bottom, learning the job from the ground up. But this time, because I had a definite plan and real drive to succeed I rapidly progressed to the point where I was able to advise clients. Financial advice is also a career where you can differentiate yourself through qualifications, and so I spent two solid years taking exams (fitted in around work and a young family) to accelerate my progress. Five years later I owned a share in a high-end financial planning business, advising clients around the country. But after a few more years, my feet started to get that familiar itch. I found that as I hit forty the things that motivated me had changed, so it was time to change tack. Again, the self-reflection that triggered my first career change was invaluable. I now split my time between financial planning and building a start-up business in the education sector.

If I could give potential career changers any useful advice it would be this: if you're thinking of making a radical change, do not underestimate how long it will take you to re-establish yourself, make sure that you have enough of a financial cushion to see it through, and don't expect the change to be the end of the journey – more likely, it's just another step.

Other options that you might consider include:

(a) Transition gradually using your existing skills

Sometimes it is possible to use your old skills to help you transition into a new field or support you in a field that doesn't pay much but you enjoy. We have worked with many people who have combined different jobs to make a portfolio career (see Part III) where each job has a specific purpose and adds different things to their lives.

Alison originally worked as a buyer for a telecommunications company. She became interested in nutrition after reading a book on the subject and enrolled on a part-time, two-year course at the Institute for Optimum Nutrition. She then started a professional practice at home while remaining in her day job. After five years she started to work at a leading complementary medicine clinic in the evenings. A year later she took voluntary redundancy from her day job and now concentrates on her work as a nutritionist.

By her own admission, Alison says one of the disadvantages of her work is her inconsistent income, but she is willing to put up with this as she enjoys being her own boss and gets huge satisfaction from helping people improve their health and well-being.

She continues to investigate work within schools and healthcare centres to provide another more constant stream of income to complement the fluctuating income from her private practice.

(b) Reduce your outgoings

Sometimes if you are at a stage in life when you are supporting just yourself, you can make the conscious choice to reduce your expenditure each month.

Kate wasn't sure what she wanted to do when she graduated with a degree in history, but when she was offered a role as a business analyst by a leading consultancy, it seemed like too good an opportunity to pass up. It was a job that was the envy of her friends, intellectually stimulating with increasing responsibility, but the 16-hour days and weekend working coupled with the patriarchal culture started to take their toll. After nearly two years and much soul-searching, she decided the job wasn't for her. She had always found that writing came easily to her and she had long been fascinated by the world of journalism, especially as several members of her family were in the field. She wanted to check whether this was a pipe dream or a reality, so she wrote to several publications asking for work experience. She obtained a work experience placement on a publication, and in recognition of her enthusiasm and natural ability, they offered to send her on a journalism course. The money was substantially less than she had earned before but the opportunity was too good to miss. She took the course and later accepted a permanent job with the publication. She still works long hours but is now doing something that she believes in and is so much happier. She is building a long-term career plan on how she can use her writing and background in journalism in new ways.

Kate's tip to other people looking to make a change in their careers is to take the plunge. You may have to be creative in making some changes to make it work, but the upside is well worth it.

(c) Realizing assets or asking for financial help

Sometimes it may be an option to borrow from friends and family or your bank, or to use your savings or sell assets to release enough money to achieve your goal.

John had to leave school at eighteen and start earning as there wasn't the money for him to go to university. He found a series of sales jobs that came relatively easily to him and he had a lifestyle that worked for him. He bought his first car, then a flat and was regularly out with his friends. Life was fine but he knew that it really wasn't enough. If he had been able to go to university, he had had dreams of going into law. He decided to test out whether he was really interested and took an evening course in A-level Law. He passed with flying colours and decided that it was a case of now or never. He sold his flat and car and persuaded his parents to let him move back in with them while he studied for his law degree and then Articles. Many people tried to talk him out of making such a major change but he was determined to at least try. He loved the course and when it came to interviewing with major law firms, he found that his previous experience gave him a high level of confidence and an advantage over his fellow students. He has now been working in law for ten years and has never been happier.

As we have said before, when you truly know what you want (i.e. your goals), our experience is that you can make it happen if you are motivated, think creatively and have patience. Only you know what you are able and prepared to do to overcome this hurdle – but it is possible.

Chapter 8
Qualifications – or the lack of them

We are often asked how important qualifications are in a job advertisement, as this can be a sticking point for many people looking to change careers. There are actually very few jobs that require you to have specific qualifications, but if you wish to be a doctor, a chartered surveyor or a lawyer, there is no getting around the fact that qualifications are necessary. If you are looking for a career change where retraining is required, find out whether it is possible to train part-time or to do the training in several tranches. This is often going to require a fairly substantial cost and time commitment, but if you are convinced that this is the route you wish to pursue, it is well worth that investment. Before you embark on retraining, do make sure you have done your informational research (see Part III) and, where possible, have been able to shadow someone in role to ensure you are heading in the right direction. For the majority of roles, however, qualifications can sometimes be negotiable, especially if you can prove that you have experience commensurate with those qualifications. An increasing number of younger job-seekers are gathering multiple degrees and qualifications and employers are not always able to judge whether this additional knowledge will truly match what is needed on a day-to-day basis in the workplace.

If you see a job advertisement that sparks your interest but lists a qualification that you don't have as a prerequisite, don't despair! It can be tempting to just send in your CV and hope for the best, but a more effective option is to address the gap and build a case that your experience, proven skills and networks are sufficient for them to meet you for an interview. Think through why you believe they have asked for the qualification – is it just a standard question or are they asking you demonstrate a capability? Can you find a way to minimize their risk in interviewing you without that specific qualification by drawing on your past work life or other similar qualifications?

Case study: Chris Penny

I did well at school – I remember surprising my teachers at five years old that I was able to navigate my way around a BBC Micro (the pillar of primary school computing in 1989) with relative ease. Like many very young idealists, I set off from a young age with a very clear idea of what I wanted to 'be when I grew up' – I wanted to be a computer systems analyst. I worked through secondary school, choosing all the right courses (ICT, electronics, etc.) and continued this through into A-levels (Computing, Economics, Communications). At the end of college I had to make a choice. I was getting itchy feet 'learning' all day and was keen to be 'doing' as soon as possible – so the choice was easy between heading to university for four more years of academia and going into some vocational training. I started an apprenticeship with a local IT company. Within three months I realized that I was not destined to work in IT at all. I spent three months in a room with no windows and some fairly socially deficient people and made a beeline for the exit. Reverting to type for an eighteen-year-old education system dropout, I went to work in a bar ... I loved it from the first minute – the people, the variety of work, the music and the freedom – but I knew it wasn't forever. I knew I was meant to do something I was proud of, make a difference and feel deeply passionate about, but wasn't sure what, when or how.

That all changed one day when I was approached by one of my bar customers, a man called John Grace, who suggested I would make an excellent car salesman. He worked locally as manager of Motorpoint, the car supermarket. At the time, the idea sounded abhorrent: a) I didn't own a fur coat, and b) I'd never smoked a cigar in my life!* However, I'd always been passionate about cars – my dad bought *Auto Trader* magazine every Thursday and we'd sit and dream together about all the cars we'd never own. My dad was a true petrol head, changing his car frequently, and I can still remember how excited I felt every time he pulled onto the drive in his latest car. Looking back, it turns out a Ford Sierra 1.8 Sapphire was never a popular car, but to me, then … it was amazing. So I left the bar and went to sell cars.

It was there I discovered that success and satisfaction in a role isn't down to ultimate capability. I was never the best car sales-person on paper, but I loved it and because I loved it, I sold cars – lots of cars. I knew I'd found my field; I wanted to stay in the automotive industry forever, indulging my passion while achieving in my job. There was one thing missing though: I was still itching – itching to make a difference in some more meaningful way. I was in a job I was enjoying but I wasn't getting that sense of pride I knew I wanted.

One thing is absolutely certain though; passion rarely goes unnoticed for long. In the last twelve years I've progressed from sales executive through a number of different roles within the industry. I now work as Brand Director for *Auto Trader* (yes, the same company that published the magazine my dad bought every week). It is now a purely digital business, one of the UK's most visited websites, with the latest and greatest tech, systems and talent. I spend my days as an ambassador for the business, helping car retailers better understand their customers and that joy they feel when they buy a car … that same joy I felt. I wouldn't trade it for any other job in the world. I do what I love, I make a difference and I feel proud every day. Ironically, it's a technology company that just happens to be involved with cars, but now I get to apply all the academic stuff I learned, in an environment I love, while doing something I'm deeply passionate about.

From my journey, my advice is simple. You may have spent your life telling yourself you are going be a brilliant dog, but one day someone will suggest you might make a good cat: don't rule it out. When you look at your life up to that point, you might find you've always been a cat, scratching posts and sitting on the lap of old people and loving every minute, you were just convincing yourself you should be a dog. I'm a cat … and it's brilliant!

*I now work to change the perception of the industry, so don't think all car salesman wear fur coats and smoke cigars now, but I did in 2004!

Chapter 9
Finding support

> Keep away from those who try to belittle your ambitions. Small people always do that, but the really great make you believe that you too can become great.
>
> *Mark Twain*

If you are someone who naturally works away at a project without needing any support or assistance, you can fast forward to the next section. If, however, you are someone who likes input from others, seeks reassurance from family and friends when you are making big decisions, or you prefer working in a team rather than on your own, this is for you.

The first thing to consider is what kind of support will work for you:

- Do you like someone to challenge you?
- Do you want someone to be unconditionally on your side and be a cheerleader as you meet your goals?
- Is there room for both challenger and cheerleader?
- During which phases of the process do you think you are most likely to need support?

You may baulk at asking your friends for help, but even superheroes have help and support. Superman has Lois Lane, Batman has Robin ... Look around at the people you know and decide who might be able to offer you the type of support you are seeking. We suggest you choose people you trust to be honest with you and have different viewpoints to get feedback and brainstorm ideas with. It's important that they encourage you when you get stuck or feel down (sadly this is likely to happen every so often, but it does pass) and can keep you to your time frame.

Having said that, remember that they will be giving subjective advice. While it is always good to gather additional support, look at it and decide whether their feedback or opinions are useful to you and you agree with them, or whether you feel that they are not helpful to you right now or you think their advice reflects their view of the world rather than your own – at the end of the day, it is the superhero who makes the ultimate decision. It is also important that you let your supporters know what works for you and what you would prefer them to do more of, if it is working, and less of, if you think it might hinder your progress.

One word of warning. Often other people – even those who are closest to you – may have a vested interest in keeping you just where you are. Well-meaning friends may say things like 'You're just lucky to have a good job', 'Nobody enjoys their work'. Meaning well doesn't make the comments any more positive. You will need energy and your self-esteem intact to progress in your career. So-called 'vampire friends' have to be managed carefully so that you don't get dragged down by them. If you don't think that certain friends are going to be positive influences as you look at your career and potentially make big changes, perhaps it might be a good idea not to dwell on the subject when you meet with them or solicit their advice, at least while you are going through this phase. Completing the exercises in this book will mean you have followed a well-thought-out methodology to deduce what you want from your work and how you are going to achieve it. This should go a long way to reassuring you that you haven't rushed into a decision.

In order to maintain momentum or if you're getting stuck, you may want to look at working with a career coach. A good coach will tell you the things you don't necessarily want to hear, challenge your thinking and encourage you to stretch yourself. It is also important, if the coaching relationship is going to be successful, that you respect one another and enjoy working together. In Part III we show you what to look out for if you do decide you want to find a career coach to work with.

If you are an organizer, something else you might consider is getting a small group of like-minded people together to work on this as a group. You can use this book as a template; do the exercises on your own and then get together weekly/monthly, or whatever works for you, to report back on progress and to share what you have discovered. You might also think about splitting the cost of a coach to facilitate the meetings with all of you – this could help to maintain the momentum and provide you with a different viewpoint.

There are always options, but for most people it is considerably easier to do this with support than on your own.

Mark credits his wife with being the impetus behind his career change and says he is quite sure that without her support and encouragement, he would still be a marketing controller, a job he hated but that paid the bills. He had talked about having his own business but the time never seemed right to make the move, so year after year passed and nothing changed. When he mentioned to his wife that his new year's resolution was to start a business, she held him to it. He had two main options – either being a marketing freelancer or a photographer, something he'd always been passionate about. In the end, he combined the two.

It eventually took Mark twenty-two months to get his business up and running, setting up a wedding photography sideline in the interim to test the market and bring in some additional income to pay for the transition. He did well and was soon winning enough work through referrals to make the business viable. He created a business plan, got himself a good accountant and joined all the professional photography organizations in his area. He used his marketing background not only to help market his own photography business but also to join forces with other complementary businesses to create a joined-up service of excellent professionals who specialize in weddings. He also works with two other businesses, one doing commercial photography and the other doing marketing consultancy.

Mark's salary is about the same as it was before and the hours are longer, but he has no doubt that his standard of living is substantially better. If it had not been the support and occasional pushing of his wife, he says he would probably still be in a role he hated, wondering 'what if'.

Bringing people with you

Making a change in career direction may have ramifications for others as well as yourself. It is vital, at the outset, to find a way to bring them with you on this journey rather than merely presenting them with a change as a done deal. Having a frank conversation with a loved one can be a major stumbling block in the process, so often the earlier those conversations take place the better.

Jordan had been working for his family's business since he left university but he had never felt particularly settled there. He worked his way through the career change exercises and made the decision to retrain as a sports injury therapist. He did all his research, spoke to therapists about their jobs and found out how he could retrain; he had even been accepted on a course. Then he came to a halt. The thing he had been avoiding was no longer avoidable. He had to tell his parents he was planning on leaving their business and would not be taking it over on their retirement. He practised the conversation over and over before finally sitting down with them and talking them through his decision. They were surprised that he had done so much without mentioning it, but after that initial surprise were wholly supportive – something he had not expected.

Bite the bullet and have the conversation. Work out what you want to say, perhaps do some research ahead of time so that you are not talking in broad brush terms about important things like how you'll be able to pay the bills, and don't be surprised if others may need some time to assimilate what you've told them. For you, this is something you have had plenty of time to think about; for them, this may come out of the blue, so give them some time to react and then think about it.

Mike had been looking for a job in his field of expertise for eighteen months following redundancy and despite his best efforts had been unsuccessful. His research and efforts had been exhaustive – he knew every employer in his field, he knew every recruiter who specialized in what he did, and he had applied for everything he could. He was stuck. During coaching, it became clear that there was 'an elephant in the room' that he was not talking about. It emerged that his wife had told him when he lost his job that he had eighteen months to find a new one or they were going to go back and live in her native Wales and become self-sufficient – Mike's idea of hell. His eighteen months were up and he was incredibly nervous and so was avoiding the conversation and deliberately being vague with his wife about his job search.

After much coaxing, he brought up the conversation and the deadline with his wife, who looked surprised and then amused. She told him that she had said what she did to try and spur him on, knowing that he would hate it; she had no intention of moving away from their lives in London if they could possibly help it. Mike felt like a huge weight had been lifted off his shoulders and returned to his job search with a different attitude. He had two job offers a month later. Clearly, that could have been a coincidence, but Mike is convinced that once that 'sword of Damocles' was no longer over his head, he came across very differently.

Whoever you feel you should bring on side in your career search, do it sooner rather than later!

Chapter 10

How to decide on a direction

A journey of a thousand miles begins with a single step.

Confucius

With so many career options available it is easy to become paralysed with indecision. Combined with the fact that there is a lot of emotion attached to choosing a new career path, it can feel like it will be difficult to make a rational, well-thought-out decision. We have spent over a decade researching and developing the methodology outlined in Parts II and III to make it as streamlined, practical and achievable as possible. We know from experience that by taking a systematic approach, gathering information, researching and under-taking due diligence, leaps of faith feel less daunting. There are many ways to dip your toe into a new field, as we saw earlier in the case study of Henry Teare, who worked at weekends and did a great deal of research to see whether his new chosen field was the right one. Working through this book will help you get enough real information about yourself, the job market you are interested in, and help you define the action steps required to make a move to minimize that risk as far as is possible. We are keen to emphasize this is a journey and often it doesn't go in a straight line from A to B but should be regarded as an ongoing process. If you are ready to take the journey with us, turn to Part II and let's start building the foundations of your new career direction.

Part II: Understanding yourself and what you want

The life that is unexamined is not worth living.

Plato

The purpose of Part II is to create a framework for your thinking and provide a structure to gather information relevant to your career. The result will give you an overview of who you are and what you want from work. Before you start protesting that you don't have time for this bit – there is no getting around the information gathering! And don't even think of outsourcing this, as only YOU know the answers! Over the years we have tested a wide variety of different exercises and the ones listed in this section have worked successfully for our clients. Often, when you are looking to change your career, you will need to do some more work on understanding yourself, so for each part we have provided some further resources to use in case you become stuck.

In Part I, we highlighted how important momentum is to success and in Part II this is going to become vital. As you complete each exercise, sorting through your work and life memories for examples, you may feel your enthusiasm waning. These exercises can be time-consuming and from experience we know that completing them is one of those things that most people tell us they are tempted to put off until tomorrow. We hate to point out the obvious, but the longer you put it off, the longer this whole process is going to take!

Follow each step of the process; you may think you already have a sense of your main skills or values, but each step has been designed as a stepping stone to the next, so it is important to follow each one through. Just like building a wall, you can count on it being the brick you have left out that will be the vital one to make the whole thing stable and useful.

The reason for gathering the information in this format is so you can pull it together in a matrix which will make up the components of the ideal job for you at this point in your life. The quality of the answers to the questions in Part II matters – in other words, the more information you gather in a clear and focused way and the more thought you put into it, the more likely you are to glean the best results. If any of the exercises seem particularly daunting, try breaking them down into manageable chunks so that you complete them, rather than feeling intimidated by what we are asking you to do or the time you think it is going to take. If you wait for that 'clear' weekend where you can sit down and do the whole lot, it may never happen! One of the things that we tell those looking to change career at the outset of the journey is that the methodology is not rocket science and that when you look back at it, much of it will feel like common sense. It has a beginning, middle and end and is based on the premise that the more real information you have, the easier it is to make decisions and move towards change.

Keep a career folder

It is a good idea to keep all the information you are going to gather in one place. It makes it easier to find all the pieces of information if you have them in a box file or virtual folder and is something many of our clients refer back to periodically as their careers develop. If you would find it easier to download printable versions of the exercises, then please go to www.howtotakechargeofyourcareer.com – where you will find all the exercises. While it is always useful to spend time **thinking** about the various aspects that we will cover in this part of the book, there is no substitute for **writing** things down, which has been proven to be so much more effective. Our clients are often surprised at how much more information they come up with when they put it down on paper.

We will look at your past and present experience, and ask you what is important to you now. We will then look at your aspirations for the future. This will all draw together to give you as complete a picture as we can get, to use as our basis for brainstorming options for your future career.

So let's kick this off by looking at what you already know from your experience to date (regardless of whether you have work experience or not!).

Chapter 11
Defining your top skills and strengths

When love and skill work together, expect a masterpiece.
John Ruskin

The starting point for any potential future employer is what skills and expertise you can bring to the role you are being interviewed for. Knowing your key skills and strengths is crucial. Perhaps more important is being able to explain the context in which you have exhibited those skills so that you can describe them in a clear and concise way. Even if you eventually set up your own business, this information will help you work out where your skill gaps are, which is crucial when hiring or partnering with other people. In this section, we are going to look at all your talents: the ones that come naturally to you and the ones you have learned. Often when we think of our skills, we refer to those that other people have told us we are good at, or we refer to our most recent job and list only those skills. We also need to be aware of the skills that we were born with, which are so often ignored.

For example, if you are naturally chatty, then it may not make sense to work in a library but you may make a fantastic radio chat show host. If you are naturally extremely organized, how can you incorporate that into your new career? What are you naturally good at doing? What do you have a knack for? We often find that these innate abilities are often overlooked and that our clients dismiss them, presuming that if they come easily to them, other people must find the same thing. It rarely occurs to us that the things that come naturally are so difficult for others, so whether you are naturally empathetic or can solve mathematical problems at the drop of the hat, it is important to recognize this.

We have found that the skills that people do well and which come easily to them often hold the clue to a future career direction. Those who incorporate these natural talents into their everyday work life are often more successful, have more confidence and enjoy what they do. Their job feels like such a natural fit and they are recognized for their excellence. Never dismiss anything that you are good at as not relevant – consider it carefully to think creatively about how you can harness what comes naturally to make it can work for you in your career, now and in the future. When we talk about someone being talented at something, we lump together a huge number of skills and strengths. Madonna can be described as a pop star, but when you break down all the aspects that this description entails, it is a long list: vocal ability, performance skills, management skills, dance skills, rhythm, entrepreneurial spirit, fashion sense, ability to reinvent oneself and stay relevant, energy, marketing skills – the list goes on. Rather than lumping together your respective talents, make sure you break them down into their component parts.

Case study: Janie Van Hool

From the age of six, I had only one life in mind. I wanted to be an actress and nothing could persuade me from focusing on this goal every waking hour until I was accepted into RADA aged nineteen. After three exhilarating years in training there, I was ready to set foot into the business and make my way. I was fortunate – I left RADA with a job, and although I didn't make my fortune, I earned enough from working across media to sustain myself as an actress and pay my bills. The thing is, it didn't turn out to be quite as I had imagined. I found filming really boring; commercials, although fantastically well paid, felt demeaning after three years of classical training and theatre meant endless travel by various unglamorous means of transport to set up in poorly attended, freezing venues for almost no money. By the time I had my children, it was apparent that Kate Winslet's career was safe – I was never going to make it big and didn't really want to settle into the 'jobbing' niche I currently occupied. I was lucky – some instinct in me had told me that at thirty, I would need a sense check. Was this the career I set out to achieve? Was I where I wanted to be? The answer for me at thirty was plainly no, so I decided to change. A chance review of a programme one night at the theatre led me to take an MA in Voice and train to teach voice and dialects to actors and in business. I now run a successful teaching practice helping people create presence and make an impact professionally.

The skills I learned as an actress are incredibly useful and I've found I can use these practical skills to make a real difference to clients, which I love. The biggest challenge I had in making the change was the grief of letting go of my childhood hopes and dreams, although I'm more successful and fulfilled now than I have ever been. It still took a couple of years to acknowledge that fact. I would definitely make a change again in the future – I'm already working towards it. My advice to anyone would be to keep reviewing: Are you where you want to be? Getting what you want? As long as you know your USP (Unique Selling Points), you can transfer your skills. It's challenging, invigorating and makes you realize what you're capable of.

Skills Exercises

Stage 1: What skills were you born with?

In addition to the more formal exercises, we have some questions for you that may just help spark an idea or thought that won't be captured in any other way. Remember to add the information from the exercise to your career folder.

Skills and talents: Things to consider

What talents do you have? What has always come easily to you at school, home, family, work, socially?

What do you most enjoy doing? What do others consider a chore but you really enjoy?

What do you find difficult that seems to come easily to other people? What are your blind spots?

Are you drawn to people or things?

Are you results orientated or do you enjoy being part of a greater whole where the final outcome is not as important to you?

Do you need to be right or are you happy working in possibilities and abstracts? Do you enjoy solving problems or prefer to avoid them?

Are you future focused?

Are you physically dexterous?

Do you like to work with other people to solve problems or by yourself?

Do you enjoy finding connections in the previously unconnected? Do you think laterally? Do you like analysing issues or solving logical puzzles?

Do you enjoy generating new ideas?

Do you use your gut feelings/intuition?

Are you a quick thinker?

Are you action orientated?

Do you enjoy working with the minutiae of a job ensuring every last 'i' is dotted or do you tend to focus on the big picture?

Are you people orientated when making decisions? Can you identify how people are feeling?

Are you more likely to analyse the logical consequences of a decision?

Are you able to adapt your style to suit someone you are engaging with?

Do you have an aptitude for languages?

Are you creative? (This can mean many things to many people, e.g. ability to think out of the box, inventive or good at generating new ideas.)

Do you have artistic ability in any form (musical, art, writing)?

Do you prefer to be organized or live in a more spontaneous way?

List the top five skills you were born with.

1

2

3

4

5

Stage 2: Proving you have those skills

This next exercise has a dual purpose. First, it will help you understand your top skills, the ones you enjoy using and would like to use in the future. Most people can do many different jobs and the challenge is to find something you enjoy. Others are able to do an excellent job despite not enjoying their work; imagine how powerful they would be if they used their skills to do something they *did* enjoy? So rather than concentrate on *all* of your skills, we will focus primarily on the ones you are good at and enjoy – a powerful combination.

Secondly, knowing and having evidence of your top skills is key to the career assessment process. For example, it's not enough to say that you have 'great communication skills', you also need to be able to answer questions such as: 'Describe a situation when you have presented ideas to a group in a persuasive manner.' This kind of question is increasingly used at interview and is called a 'competency-based' or 'behavioural' interview question. It can be difficult for an interviewer to work out competencies like 'communications skills' from CVs, as your experience can only allude to the skill and in most cases there won't be any hard evidence.

Step 1
Think of times in your life when you have really enjoyed doing something and been good at it – the times when

you felt immersed in what you were doing and were proud of the results. Jog your memory by getting out an old CV, listing all the jobs you have ever done (paid and not paid) or looking back through photograph albums. What did you get commended for, both inside and outside work? What did you really enjoy doing? Also think back over your home life and education in the same way, and analyze your achievements. If very little comes to you at first, write down as much as you can, then leave it and come back to it – take your time. Try to think of actual examples and give as much detail as possible. We ask you to analyse these stories in this format as it is how many recruiters want to see evidence of your skills.

Competency-based questions

When answering competency-based interview questions, it is useful to use the STAR method which stands for:

S – Situation – give the context in which you used your skills

T – Task – what was the challenge?

A – Action – what was the action you took?

R – Result – what was the result?

In an interview, you can tell when it is a competency-based question as it usually starts with the words, 'Tell me about a time when you ...', 'Describe a situation when you have ...', Give me an example of when you have ...'

Below is an example of how you would do this. We have chosen an example which is non-work related as it is always important to think about these events in your life too.

What was the Situation? My best friend's birthday.

What was the Task you had to undertake? Organize her birthday party without her knowledge.

What was the Action you took?
Contacted a small group of friends/her family to agree on the type of party, location, how we were going to pay for it and the guest list.

Sent out invitations to everyone she would want at the event, having 'obtained' her address book and social networking contacts.

Arranged for overnight accommodation for guests who needed it.

Found a venue and organized entertainment for the night (including music, food, drink, photographer, transport to and from the event).

Devised an intricate plan to get her to the party without her realizing what was going on (including arranging an outfit, makeover, etc.) so that she would arrive feeling like a million dollars.

Sorted out the finance for the event and made sure everyone knew what they would have to contribute ahead of time so this aspect ran smoothly.

Acted as MC for the event and arranged speeches and a slide show of pictures from her past.

Following the event, put together a book of photographs of the evening as her final present.

What was the Result you got? It was a fantastic party that everyone enjoyed. My friend was very touched and excited to have a birthday party arranged for her. She couldn't believe that she had absolutely no idea what was going on until she arrived.

If you are struggling to come up with ideas for this section then you could ask a friend or family member who might help to jog your memory, encourage you and give an objective viewpoint.

Pick five stories of your own using the STAR method. You can fill in your first one here:

Story 1

What was the Situation?

What was the Task you had to undertake?

What was the Action you took?

What was the Result you got?

James found this exercise a struggle: 'I had been warned that this would take me quite a while to do but it was hard to find the motivation to keep going. I struggled to come up with a list of things I was proud of having achieved and then deciding which stories to expand was difficult – was I getting it right? I'm pleased I stuck with it though because although the list wasn't hugely different to a general skills list I would have pulled together myself, having stories to back up those skills has proved invaluable in interview situations. The hard work was worth it.'

Step 2

Go through the following list of skills for each story and ask yourself the question: 'Can I prove that I have acquired these skills in each situation?' If so, tick the corresponding box. Once you have done the initial review, you can refine the list, especially if you find that for a particular situation, you have ticked several words that effectively mean the same thing.

For each story – I displayed the ability to:

Skill	Place a tick by each of the skills in which you think you have a strength and which enjoy.
Act	
Adapt	
Administrate	
Advertise	
Analyse	
Arbitrate	
Assist	
Assess	
Audit	
Brainstorm	
Budget	
Business development	
Business relationships	
Calculate	
Change management	
Coach	
Collaborate	
Communicate in writing	
Communicate verbally	
Communicate fluently in a foreign language	
Compile	

Compose	
Compute	
Conceptualize	
Conduct	
Conservation	
Consolidate	
Consult	
Contract	
Construct	
Contribute	
Coordinate	
Delegate	
Deliver	
Demonstrate	
Design	
(be) Detail orientated	
Develop ideas	
Discover	
Distribute	
Document	
Draft	
Educate	
Empathize	
Employ	
Examine	
Enforce	
Engineer	
Enhance	
Entertain	

Establish	
Entrepreneurship	
Evaluate	
Event organization/ management	
Execute	
Experiment	
Explain	
Explore	
Facilitate	
Finance	
Forecast	
Formulate	
Fundraise	
Gather information	
Generate ideas	
Give appropriate feedback	
Handle complaints	
Handle details	
Identify problems	
Identify resources	
Illustrate	
Implement	
Improve	
Improve processes	
Improvise	
Influence	
Innovate	
Inspect	

Inspire	
Interpret	
Interview	
Invent	
Investigate	
Keep detailed records	
Judge	
Lead	
Learn	
Listen	
Make decisions	
Market	
Manage a team	
Manage change	
Manage conflict	
Manage time	
Manage information	
Mediate	
Mentor	
Model	
Monitor	
Motivate	
Multitask	
Negotiate	
Network	
Observe	
Organize	
Overhaul	
Partner with	

Perceive patterns	
Pioneer	
Planning	
Persuade verbally	
Persuade in writing	
Predict	
Present	
Prioritize	
Problem solve	
Programme management	
Project management	
Promote change	
Publicize	
Question	
Reason	
Recommend	
Recruit	
Repair	
Research	
Review	
Relationship building	
Save time	
Save money	
Save resources	
Sell ideas	
Sell products	
Set goals	
Set and meet deadlines	
Standardize	

Support others	
Teach	
Team build	
Think laterally	
Train	
Volunteer	
Other:	
Other:	
Other:	
Other:	
Other:	

Which are the skills which get the highest number of ticks? List the top five here:

1

2

3

4

5

Step 3: Consolidate your findings

Referring to the five skills above, write a sentence that details your real and specific strengths. For example, you may state communication as one of your top skills – but what makes you stand out is your ability to communicate clearly and in a motivational way in tough situations. This can help you work out where to focus this skill.

My strength in skill 1 is:

My strength in skill 2 is:

My strength in skill 3 is:

My strength in skill 4 is:

My strength in skill 5 is:

We ask you to consider your skills in this way as it highlights when your answer is too vague and really makes you think about the evidence of your top skills. There may be some crossover between your 'born skills' and these skills you have solid evidence for – that's fine. It's important to look at them all.

Finally, it is important to consider your skills in relation to the market:

Do your skills have long-term currency as you progress in your career or might you need to develop these skills further?

Are your skills becoming obsolete in the market?

Chapter 12

What do you value?

Live your beliefs and you can turn the world around.

Henry David

When we start to explore what people value in their lives and work environments, we often find this is something that most have spent little, if any, time thinking about. While they recognize that knowing what is important to them is key, values are something that most of us don't build into the equation when we are looking at careers, but our values can serve as a useful focus or reference point for all aspects of our life.

We define work values as 'those interests and qualities which you feel are important in your work'. Obviously your work values are highly likely to overlap with your personal values, but it is useful to have a think about whether your life is aligned with the things you say are important to you. This is one area which can change radically as you have more life experiences or life changes (e.g. having a family to consider).

It may not be necessary to orient your life entirely around your values; however, it will be possible (and rewarding) to weave them into most aspects of your life.

Acting as a reference point, values can help you to:

- set clear goals for the future that are worthwhile and are important to you.
- improve the quality of your decisions.
- maintain your confidence when you feel confused or when you're in a period of transition.

We suggest you redo this exercise every year. Your values can change with your life circumstances so it is important to ensure that your life is in line with your current values rather than those of five years ago.

Values Exercise

Step 1

Tick any 10 values from these groups of values that naturally appeal to you; if you can't find the right words, add your own so that they reflect you as closely as possible.

AFFILIATION

- ☐ Co-operation
- ☐ Sociability
- ☐ Closeness
- ☐ Warmth
- ☐ Family
- ☐ Affection
- ☐ Friendship
- ☐ Camaraderie
- ☐ Affiliative

AUTONOMY

- ☐ Autonomy
- ☐ Personal Authority
- ☐ Independence

ALTRUISM

- ☐ Tolerance
- ☐ Care
- ☐ Guidance
- ☐ Nurture
- ☐ Empathy
- ☐ Support
- ☐ Development
- ☐ People Orientated
- ☐ Altruistic

CREATIVITY

- ☐ Individuality
- ☐ Unpredictability
- ☐ Expedience
- ☐ Originality
- ☐ Ingenuity
- ☐ Freedom
- ☐ Creativity

ENTREPRENEURIAL

- ❏ Risk
- ❏ Adventure
- ❏ Experiment
- ❏ Dynamism
- ❏ Competition
- ❏ Energy
- ❏ Innovation
- ❏ Novelty
- ❏ Entrepreneurial zeal

EXPERTISE

- ❏ Expertise
- ❏ Technical Expertise
- ❏ Proficiency
- ❏ Superiority
- ❏ Competence

INTELLECT

- ❏ Education
- ❏ Intellectually Challenging
- ❏ Intellectual stimulation

LIFESTYLE/WORK BALANCE

- ❏ Lively
- ❏ Fun
- ❏ Choice
- ❏ Flexibility
- ❏ Good work/life balance

FINANCIAL REWARD

- ❏ Profit
- ❏ Pay and bonuses
- ❏ Financial freedom
- ❏ Building financial value

POWER AND INFLUENCE

- ❏ Guidance
- ❏ Governance
- ❏ Influence

RECOGNITION

- ❏ Respect
- ❏ Reward
- ❏ Praise
- ❏ Recognition
- ❏ Appreciation

SECURITY

- ❏ Predictability
- ❏ Safety
- ❏ Security
- ❏ Stability
- ❏ Regularity

STRUCTURE

- ❏ Structure
- ❏ Organisation
- ❏ Order
- ❏ Clarity
- ❏ Efficiency

YOUR OWN

- ❏
- ❏
- ❏
- ❏
- ❏

Figure 2.1

Step 2

Now that you have your preliminary list (your ticked 'values'), this will help you to rank your values in order of importance.

List your 10 values in the column on the left hand side of the grid on the page (see page 84 for a blank Deciding Values Grid). To decide which value is most important, compare each pair of values and circle the number relating to the value you decide on. When arriving at your decision ask yourself: If I could only say one of these was true for my chosen career, which would I prefer? Try not to think what others might say or think about you – be brutally honest with yourself.

Once you have completed the whole grid, you need to add up the number of times you have circled each value and enter it in the corresponding box in the 'number of circles' line at the bottom of the grid.

This will help you determine the ranking of your values. Allocate 1–10 to your values according to the number of times you have circled them across the whole grid.

Enter the rankings into the 'final ranking' line at the bottom of the grid. You can now enter your prioritized values in the right-hand column of the grid.

These can be used as your reference point for any job-hunting activities or career decisions you are required to make.

For a completed example of the Deciding Values Grid, see page 83. Then complete your own on page 84.

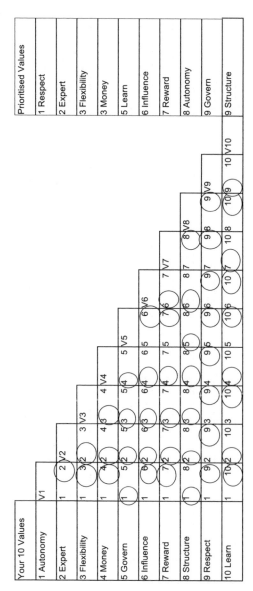

Your 10 Values											Prioritised Values
1 Autonomy	V1										1 Respect
2 Expert	1	2 V2									2 Expert
3 Flexibility	1	3 2	3 V3								3 Flexibility
4 Money	1	4 2	4 3	4 V4							3 Money
5 Govern	1	5 2	5 3	5 4	5 V5						5 Learn
6 Influence	1	6 2	6 3	6 4	6 5	6 V6					6 Influence
7 Reward	1	7 2	7 3	7 4	7 5	7 6	7 V7				7 Reward
8 Structure	1	8 2	8 3	8 4	8 5	8 6	8 7	8 V8			8 Autonomy
9 Respect	1	9 2	9 3	9 4	9 5	9 6	9 7	9 8	9 V9		9 Govern
10 Learn	1	10 2	10 3	10 4	10 5	10 6	10 7	10 8	10 9	10 V10	9 Structure

1	2	3	4	5	6	7	8	9	10	Item number
2	8	6	6	1	4	3	1	9	5	Number of circles
#8	#2	#3	#3	#9	#6	#7	#9	#1	#5	Final Rank

Figure 2.2 Example of deciding values

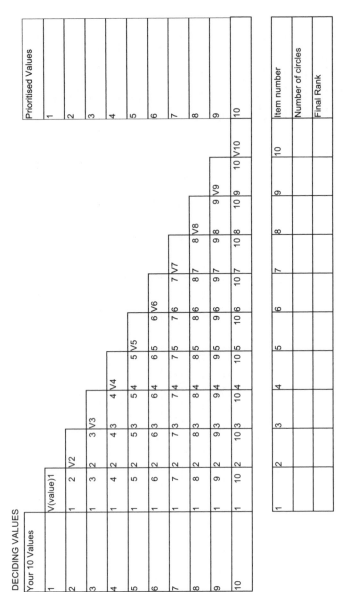

Figure 2.3 Example of deciding values

Chapter 13
What are your interests and passions?

Let the beauty of what you love be what you do.

Rumi

Interests can be a major factor in your career. They can help you decide which industry to target or what type of business to set up. Working in an industry or business which incorporates your interests can make you feel motivated to work harder, and usually results in increased job satisfaction. Having said that, sometimes interests should stay as hobbies! Perhaps there is no way to make them commercially viable, or maybe they bring in some income but not enough to support you full time. A lot of the people we work with don't know what they are really interested in. It is very important to start to become more aware of what holds your interest (i.e. having an 'explorer's mindset') and what bores you to tears. This is different for different people – while racing cars might fascinate you, it may bore me. With our recruiter's hat on, we can see when someone is passionate about what they do: their eyes sparkle, they are animated when talking about it, and the energy just radiates from them. Often this passion will set them apart from the rest and when employed, they will have the energy to go the 'extra mile' and give 100 per cent to everything they do. It may take some soul-searching and time to find industries you are interested in, but it is time well spent as it will mean your career often has more longevity.

So how do you get in touch with what you are interested in and then evaluate whether it should form part of your career plan? First you need to increase your awareness and the first step is to answer the questions below.

Interests exercise

Answer the questions below and consider whether your interests could form part of your career. Try to be as specific as you can. If business interests you, what part of business? Sales? Human Resources? Try to break it down further – if it is Human Resources, is it recruitment, compensation and benefits or training?

The last couple of questions focus around industry sector. We ask these questions because it helps to also target industry sectors you are interested in that may be growing, thus offering more opportunity.

1   What do you do in your leisure time?
2   Are you passionate about any of your interests?
3   Do you have knowledge or relative expertise in an area that you have built up just because you are interested in it?
4   What books, blogs or magazines do you read? If you went into a bookshop, what sections would you look in?
5   What subjects do you follow on social media such as Twitter, Instagram, YouTube?
6   What section of the newspaper do you turn to first?
7   Have you ever volunteered for work or assignments?
8   Are you interested in any particular industry sector?
9   Which industry sectors do you think are growing or have potential for growth?

It can be useful to keep coming back to this section and adding things that pique your interest. Add articles to your career folder. Keep a note of films, TV or radio programmes that make you think and interest you – what is it about them that caught your interest? Some people can be downhearted if they can't seem to find that one thing that really ignites their passion. This is not unusual but don't give up. Keep looking out for fields that pique your interest and do some research to find out more about them – it can sometimes be an aspect to the field that you haven't come across before that contains the key to a new direction. Look at anything that interests you – is it cooking desserts, researching holiday destinations or finding out about family history? Start researching options that might work with those interests and you might be able to creatively combine different fields of interest in your work and personal life perhaps by adopting a portfolio career.

George was always passionate about music. He was the founder and Music Director of the College when he was at university. After a degree in Natural Sciences, he went into the City as a financial analyst at Hill Samuel. Following an MBA from Tuck School of Management he joined Cargill, in the food production industry, as a senior manager and eventually became a director responsible for Strategy for Business Development. With a young family, he was tired of travelling constantly and in his mind he had a burning desire to combine his skills with his first love – music.

After following the career change process, he made the big decision to move to be Head of Commercial Development at Glyndebourne Opera. This has necessitated a lifestyle change for George, but with his family supporting his decision, he successfully made the transition and is utilizing his business skills in a field he is passionate about.

Finding evidence of your passion

It is all very well to say you are 'passionate' about a field, but you need to gather your evidence that it is a viable option – not only for the employer if you are going for interview, but also for yourself if you are changing career. George could draw on a lifelong interest in music evidenced by his early achievements at university.

From our experience as recruiters and those we speak to regularly, the importance of collecting evidence of your interest in a new career is key. This may include some of the following:

- Unpaid work or voluntary work full-time, part-time or in your spare time – you don't have to say it was unpaid on your CV!
- Consultancy or contract work to gain experience.
- Involvement in clubs or associations connected with your interest.

Case study: Robert Timothy

I landed in London about twelve years ago from South Africa with a suitcase of clothes, some savings and not much else. I guess I thought I was a boy with a big dream, but to be honest, I didn't have a clue what that dream was! I'd been working in radio in Cape Town and I thought the best way to progress my career would be to spend a few years in the media in the UK. I had fallen into the radio job after someone heard me on university radio (then just a hobby to avoid going to lectures) and I was made an employment offer I couldn't refuse. But now I was in London with a dwindling savings balance and still not quite sure how my amazing career was going to progress. 'But I'll get a job to pay the rent and then I'll figure it out …' I had a friend who had an 'in' at Sky News and it seemed a good idea. 'I'll spend a few months there while I work out exactly what it is I want to do …' And then I saw an ad for broadcast journalists at the BBC. 'Oh, the BBC. There will be loads of opportunities. I should go there …'

Fast forward nearly a decade and I'm waiting in line to view the body of Nelson Mandela as he lay in state in Pretoria. I was back in the country on assignment, to produce coverage of his funeral for BBC News. That's when I had The Moment. As I stepped forward to the coffin and saw Madiba lying there – an icon of mine and one of our time – a thought flashed into my head: 'So Robert, what did you do with YOUR life?' It took the death of a hero to make me realize that my life had been happening while I was not even making plans but making plans to make plans. Sound familiar?

Four months later I was back in London, working my last day as staff after ten years at the BBC. I'd fallen into the wrong career by accident and I had to change. But to what?

Being a teenager in Cape Town in the 1990s was a heady experience. Our country was the toast of the planet and it felt like the world had come to join the fun, including the fashion industry. Photographers would jet in with $10,000-a-day supermodels and designers in tow, to shut off an entire road for a photoshoot. Seeing this, as a sixteen-year-old, in my wildest dreams, what would have been my absolute dream job?

Today I'm glad to tell you that my photos have been published in various magazines and have even hung at the National Portrait Gallery in London. I work with the world's top modelling agencies in some of the most beautiful locations. I haven't yet shut off a street, although we did bring the traffic to a standstill on Ocean Drive in Miami.

I ended up in the wrong career by accident and I made the change. News journalism to fashion photography is not a path well trodden, but life is too short to be doing the wrong job. It's hard not to resort to slogans, but the best way I can sum it up is: 'Find your passion, make it happen'. Passion is the faith you need to persist.

There have been times when I've felt overwhelmed and scared, but nothing is as frightening as the thought of regret and not making the change. Whatever you can do, do it now – and if you're in the wrong career, change it.

Find a way to get your foot in the door

Working with a career coach, Steve identified the key skills that would be attractive to an employer and the subjects that he was passionate about. When combined, Steve's research pointed to a career in the commercial side of the sports industry. It was a small field and operated on a 'who you know' basis. Through leveraging his limited contacts to make new ones, Steve eventually secured his first role at a sports management company for six months, which was the foot in the door he needed.

People working as a consultant or on a contract are very attractive to employers, as they are a much lower risk hire than those joining the firm through traditional recruitment channels like advertising. Employers have seen first hand the quality of their work and how they fit into the team – the best 'interview' there is! It also means the employer saves substantially on recruitment fees, which can vary from anything between 15–33 per cent of annual salary.

Complete a course or enhance your knowledge about your field

Charlotte had gone into interior design after a history degree at university. She found interior design stifling and realized it didn't stretch her intellectually. Not knowing what she wanted to do, frustrated and confused as to what career to follow, she went travelling, but returned a year later no further on in her thinking. After completing the skills exercise (see above), she discovered that while she had been working in interior design she had particularly enjoyed putting client records onto a database she had designed. She had a fledging interest in IT and decided to do a six-week evening course to see if this interest was just a passing phase or something more substantial. After the course, she discovered her interest had grown and she felt motivated to move into this field. She received several offers from IT graduate recruitment schemes, despite, at twenty-seven, being older than the majority of people on such schemes. She accepted an offer from Thames Water and the HR Manager who interviewed her said one of the main reasons the company offered her the job is that she had clearly worked through a structured career assessment and they felt she had done her 'career change' homework. She was not a 'risk' because she had proven evidence of her interest in the IT field.

Charlotte took a short course to test her interest in a field that was relatively new to her. Attending events such as conferences and reading the industry press can help ensure you come across as knowledgeable; we have known several people who have been hired after meetings at industry events. This insider's knowledge can improve the questions you ask and make you appear to have been in the industry for ages. Once you have overcome this initial hurdle of making contact and appearing to be knowledgeable about the industry you are seeking to join, then sometimes a lack of experience can be overlooked.

Include project work as part of your course if you are doing a further education qualification

Many MBA and Master's students use projects and internships to gain experience which then serves as that vital evidence of interest in a new field. Sometimes projects can be carefully planned so that there is an opportunity to talk to different companies and to people who could potentially hire you.

Robin used his MBA project in internal change management at a major oil company to make the transition into consultancy. While working on the project, he came into contact with several consultancy firms; he interviewed with a couple before finally joining one of them. Since then he has transferred to the Perth office to combine his management consultancy career with the outdoor lifestyle he had identified as a passion.

If you are an undergraduate, there may be ways to use your dissertation or placement year in the same way.

Travel

Many people take gap years or travel breaks, often as an escape from a job or because they are not sure what to do next. Undertaken carefully, travel can help you to gain experience in a certain field. For example, working on an English newspaper in a foreign country might be useful if you are looking to gain journalism experience. If you do go travelling, future employers may want to know what you got out of it, so it's always useful to keep that in mind – what experiences might show a new aspect of your personality or a key area of competence?

Tom didn't enjoy being a solicitor and had originally planned to go travelling to 'escape' his solicitor job. After working through these exercises, he decided to pursue his interest in wine and used his travel time in Australia to do some research into the wineries there. He spent several months talking to people in the trade and researching the types of roles available in the industry. He came back even more determined to enter the wine trade. He sold his house to release some equity to live on while he took a radical pay cut to work in a local wine shop to gain experience at the same time as he took his wine exams. Over the years, he has steadily progressed within the wine trade and despite the drop in income compared with a career in the law, he has never regretted his move.

Some people, such as Christine Rucker from The White Company, have developed a business around their passion – in her case, interior design. For others this can be a mistake. Just because you love golf, for example, doesn't necessarily mean you would love running a golfing shop – the day-to-day running of a shop or even a chain of shops is not necessarily the same as the buzz you get from playing or watching golf on TV. This is why it is important to consider your interests and passions not in isolation but in relation to the other career elements such as skills, values, work environments, etc. You may be able to weave interests and hobbies into your life in other ways – for example, Mark decided that while he was passionate about climbing and skiing in the mountains, the types of full-time roles open to him would not meet his financial requirements. He ended up relocating to New Zealand but staying in the same field of IT, which allowed him to also pursue his passion for mountain sports.

Case study: Lindsay Small

Although I went to a good university, I found academic study very frustrating. I wanted to be out in the world, and at that time 'the City' was the place to be. I took the secretarial route into the City, then managed to move from that into investment research – writing my own research as an analyst and then editing other people's research. Editing quickly became a passion; I was good at it, and I loved the City environment. It was my decision to have children that provoked a career change. I wasn't prepared to work full-time City hours, and in those days there wasn't any leeway.

Although it was my decision, I found life at home with the kids a real challenge at first; I was a fish out of water in the playground and I missed almost everything about the City. To maintain my interests over the next few years, I started three small businesses. It was the start-up phase which really interested me; they never held my interest once they were up and running. They brought in a little income and experience, but most importantly, I learned something about myself and my strengths and weaknesses with each new venture, and that process ultimately allowed me to discover my perfect business – the internet. Almost the first time I went online I realized that I had found my perfect field. When my youngest child started school I began to work on a website for parents and teachers of young children. It took off very quickly, and now, over fifteen years later, some 1.5 million people visit the website every month. I work from home, helped by a small band of freelancers, and I earn a very good income. I still find new challenges to keep me interested and motivated, and am able to work completely around my family.

Would I change my career again? Absolutely, as long as I was working for myself! There are so many things that I would like to have a go at, and I still have new ideas almost every day. These days so many people get stuck in one unfulfilling career because firms want specialists, and good specialists are encouraged to stay in that speciality forever. But that doesn't mean you can't do something else – or 100 other things, given the time and the inclination! And if your first attempt isn't perfect for you, learn from it, examine your strengths and weaknesses, and move onto the next …

Chapter 14

What is your ideal working environment?

> The words printed here are concepts. You must go through the experiences.
>
> *Saint Augustine*

You now have a comprehensive list of your transferable skills, values and interests to capitalize on in your next role. Continuing the theme of looking to what you know about yourself from experience, next we are going to look at common themes that have surfaced about what you like and dislike in a work environment. Don't panic if you don't have a huge amount of work experience to draw upon – any information is useful. Many of us will have been in an environment that was toxic to us and not conducive to doing our best work. It's very important that you take the time to recognize which environment to avoid in the future and which to seek out. This focus can be of interest to potential employers who, in our experience, are impressed by someone who has taken the time to ensure they are joining the right environment for them – a form of due diligence. It shows you take your career seriously and you understand the best environment for you. We also know that potential employers and recruiters are impressed when a candidate had taken the time to speak to other people in the firm to find out what it is really like to work there. This reduces the risk of a candidate joining and then leaving as there isn't a good 'fit' – making the recruiter and the candidate look good.

Environment Exercise

For each job you have held in the past, describe as fully as possible those factors which made that job especially exciting or rewarding (i.e. those things you liked) and those elements that made that job especially boring or frustrating (i.e. things you disliked). Be as specific as possible.

Examples to consider might include:

Office (was it open plan, did you have your own office, was it light and airy).

Colleagues (were they social, interactive, team orientated, quiet).

Remuneration (pay, benefits such as holiday, canteen, pension).

Promotion prospects.

Sense of freedom (did you work out of the office, were you micromanaged).

Style of management (open to suggestion, hierarchical, collegiate, supportive).

Development (were development opportunities offered, e.g. coaching, mentoring, training).

Why are you (thinking about) no longer working there?

What was it about the role that made you want to take it on?

How did it live up to expectations?

How did it fail to live up to expectations?

Do you thrive in a big company environment? Would you be better suited to a smaller company?

JOB	LIKED	DISLIKED

When Megan first did this exercise, she did a quick download of information so she could get to the next section. When she came to review it later, she started to see the first signs of some common themes, such as having autonomy in her work life, not being tied to her job 9–5, being with sparky individuals who believed in something. This was where she started her brainstorming and she's now working with an SME where there is huge freedom to contribute to a product they all feel passionately about.

Your ideal environment

This list of likes and dislikes should give you an idea of what to look for and what to avoid when you are considering approaching certain firms. Take the three most important elements of your ideal work environment and list them below.

1

2

3

Case study: Anne Williams

The turning point came for me when I returned to work after the birth of my first child, as a project manager for a high-profile strategic redesign business improvement project. This gave me exposure to management consultants and I instinctively knew this was far more 'me'. At that time my world was one-dimensional and it was then that I intuitively understood that I needed to complete an MBA to equip me with the skills for a future career challenge and change. After several false starts post MBA, where I ended up working for organizations with work environments that ignored bad management practices, I learnt that at interview it was crucial for me to go into a lot of detail about an average day to make a decision about whether it was right for me – just because they want you doesn't mean the job's right for you! I am now about to start working for one of the world's top five management consultancies.

Will it work for me? I think so, but why do I believe that I have got it right this time? First, I was overtly 'me' during the recruitment process, which entailed four one-to-one interviews, three psychometric tests and a role play, in an attempt to test the boundaries of the personality/culture fit. This didn't seem to set off any alarm bells, if anything it was the reverse. The more I came out of my shell, the more successful I was. It appears that my critical insight was an asset not a threat; my intellect and academic achievement an advantage not a hindrance; my gregarious nature and sense of fun a key tool in networking and maintaining visibility rather than a distraction and a nuisance. Will it work? Who really knows but I think it will. Many of my colleagues and friends are keen to point out to me that this is exactly what I should have done years ago, that it 'suits' me and my skills best. Either way, I am not worried anymore, because I know that if it is not me, I am good enough and the search must go on. All that it needed, like finding your lifetime partner, is that 'right fit'. My one piece of advice is: always strive for that perfect personal 'fit', to have the confidence to craft and shape your life, being uncompromising and constantly questioning – so you can get the best out of it!

Chapter 15

Your relationship with previous managers

'I hate my boss!' is a familiar refrain for most people at some point during their working life. A great manager can support you, coach and develop you to be the best you can be. On the other hand, a nightmare boss can belittle you, undermine you and wreck your confidence. You may have mentioned your previous bosses/managers in the exercise you have just done, but we want you to explore this a little more. Identifying why you didn't get on with certain managers and what traits you need in your manager to bring out the best in you is an important consideration when you are looking for a new role. If you've ever had a bad manager, you'll know exactly what we are talking about – they can make or break a job, as many of our clients (us included!) have unfortunately found out.

Relationship with managers exercise

List below all the managers you have had in the past.

1

2

3

4

5

(add more if needed)

When you look at that list, who did you work well for? Who would you cross the street to avoid now? Why? Knowing what you know about working for them, list the positive characteristics you are looking for in your next manager and list the negative characteristics you are seeking to avoid:

Positive	Negative
e.g. supportive, clever, inclusive, fun, role model	e.g. megalomaniac, moody, closed, micromanager

When Karen did this exercise, she was fascinated and surprised to see a common theme in the types of people she had worked for (all power-hungry alpha personalities) who had never made her feel like she could achieve but were charismatic when she met them. When she was interviewing, she was offered two roles, She found it incredibly difficult to decide which way to go until she revisited this exercise. One of the roles would have involved working with another similar boss, the other was working for someone who was more focused on developing her in her new role. That was her decider and she didn't regret it.

Finding out whether the environment or your manager is a good fit for you is down to your investigative abilities! You need to talk to people who work for the company, perhaps a friend of a friend who works there or, even better, someone who used to work there as they may be able to be more honest. LinkedIn is useful for this research. Another way to check this out is to ask to meet the team for lunch or drinks after you have accepted an offer. That way you can ask some informal questions about the working environment to see if it really is for you.

Chapter 16
Taking care of your needs

To know oneself, one should assert oneself.

Albert Camus

So far, the majority of Part II has looked at what we would like in an ideal working world: the skills we would like to use, the types of people we would like to work with, and so on. The one thing we must be careful not to overlook is our own needs.

In 1943, Abraham Maslow developed his Hierarchy of Needs (see Figure 2.4). As human beings, we start with our most

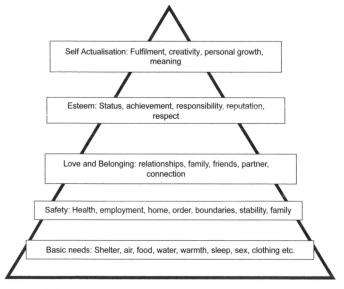

Figure 2.4

basic needs at the bottom of the triangle and as we achieve each level of needs, we move up to the next one. It is perfectly possible to be moving through a couple of the levels at any one time. Where do you consider yourself to be right now? Are you striving to move to the higher levels and do you have a plan of how you hope to do that?

In terms of your next career move, have you considered what it is you *need* in order to make your next move more likely to work?

Needs exercise

Mark below the five main needs that you would like your future career to fulfil. Things you might want to consider are:

- job security
- location
- salary (give a range – both the minimum you can afford initially and the amount that will put a smile on your face)
- any working constraints (hours you can work, ability to travel, etc.)
- recognition
- promotion prospects.

1

2

3

4

5

After working out his budget and looking at all possible options, Peter knew he needed a certain basic salary to be able to keep up with his everyday bills such as mortgage, utilities, food, etc. and without it he knew he would be panic-stricken and struggle to function, even in a job he thought he would love. So he applied for, and got, a reduction of hours in his corporate job that would cover his main expenses and which left him with two days a week to pursue his new career as an upholsterer. Peter feels secure financially and is able to slowly build up his upholstery business. Although this has meant sacrificing potential career progression in his corporate role, it gives him an opportunity to check out the viability of his new career in a way that feels safe for him. Peter was honest about what his needs really were and adapted his plans to work for him. He had carefully considered what he would compromise on and what, categorically, he couldn't, which helped him make an informed decision.

Chapter 17

What do I want out of life? Defining your long-term plan

> Be not afraid of going slowly, be afraid only of standing still.
>
> *Chinese Proverb*

So far, we have looked at what you can learn from your past experiences and your present reality to help build up a picture of what you are looking for in your ideal career path. Now we will look at your aspirations for the future and make sure that you are looking forward to feature your hopes and dreams.

Clearly, nothing is written in stone. Life happens and your aspirations and hopes for the future will change through circumstances both positive and negative. What we are looking for here is a snapshot from where you are right now of what you hope to achieve, not only in your career but in your life as a whole. Identifying your hopes for the future may help with the brainstorming of possible job options (see Chapter 19 below) and your aspirations may highlight a new path to explore.

John had been in accounting for ten years. He was bored and the idea of the rest of his career doing more of the same with a few promotions along the way was demoralizing. Having worked through all the exercises up to this point, a new direction was still not showing itself and he was starting to lose hope that he would find the right role – until, that is, he started looking into the future. He went through the next exercise filling in the information for each ten-year period until he wrote up his aspirations for his fifties. Seemingly out of nowhere, his new career was to own a bistro with an art gallery attached where he could introduce his local community to young artists. However, in discussion, he said he felt it would only be possible to do that when he had made enough money to do what he really wanted as a 'hobby job'. As soon as he said it, the light bulb went on! He had found what he really wanted to do – now it was just a question of how to make it happen sooner. He had been persuaded by well-meaning teachers and parents to take up science rather than art at school and had never really considered the creative world as a possible job option, although he still painted watercolours in his spare time. After much research and helping out at a local art gallery and museum at weekends, he retrained as an art restorer and is now working in an art gallery as a curator.

Sometimes releasing the pressure of an immediate plan can show up some interesting ideas that you have played with in the back of your mind for years but have never thought possible. Now is the time to put that theory to the test through research and exploration to find out whether your idea is a pipe dream or could be reality.

Most of us, when we talk about the future, tend not to think too far ahead – five years being the norm for those who have spent some time building long-term goals. Our clients rarely look at how their long-term perspectives will change as they become older, perhaps move to the country, change their social habits. This section asks you to consider how old you will be, how old your possible children will be and to really put yourself in that place to answer the questions.

Case study: Gordon Green

My first job was in the graduate programme of a major oil company after successfully completing a Chemical Engineering degree at university. I had no specific plan at the time and the programme certainly lived up to its reputation – I had assignments and gained valuable experience in many different parts of the organizations, coupled with lots of travelling internationally and working very closely with the senior management. I thoroughly enjoyed my first few years but it was a double-edged sword, as I began to feel that I wasn't in control of where my career was going – I was expected to move to different departments and locations at short notice and with no input. Sensing my restlessness, the company sponsored me to do an MBA. Through the MBA, I met many like-minded people and started to have the confidence to shape my own career, instead of just allowing it to 'happen'. My goal was to be self-employed so I would be able to choose my own lifestyle. But it also had to be a job which could bring me more satisfaction, in terms of tangible benefits to someone's life, and not just helping an organization to be more profitable. And that's when I decided to be a lawyer. But to get there I would need to be financially secure as I appreciated the risks involved. So when I graduated from my MBA, I went into investment banking; being an investment banker not only provided enough mental challenges, but it also taught me how to work in an ultra-competitive environment with some of the brightest brains around.

I thoroughly enjoyed my time in investment banking and the adrenalin rush that accompanied it. But more importantly, I saved every penny of my bonuses in those few years, as I knew it was an important step in my plan. I did have my moment of doubt when I left investment banking – everybody was questioning the sanity of my decision. Why would one walk away from such a coveted job, with its pay and prestige? But I knew what I had in mind, so I started doing my legal training part-time, while using my previous experience in banking to get a job in a law firm, albeit in a non-legal capacity. I undertook four years of part-time studying while working full-time in one of the largest law firms in the world. It was not the easiest thing to do but it was all worth it, as my future employer could see my seriousness in making a career change. So now I am well on my way to finishing my training to be a lawyer, and will soon to be able to work in an area I am interested in – human rights.

Looking back, I think one thing I have learned is that whatever you are doing now – and it may be something you do not enjoy – there are bound to be qualities/experience which will help you move on to the next step, so it's important not to just focus on that goal you have in mind while missing out on the lessons you can learn in your current situation. The other important area is to have patience – it's very easy to walk away from what you don't like and hope to make a complete change overnight. But it's equally important to bear in mind that many goals take a lot of planning and time to achieve; don't be put off by discouraging people who tell you that you'll be starting from the bottom of the ladder again, you'll be older than most, etc. These are usually people who are too afraid to make a change themselves.

Having an idea of your long-term goals will keep you focused on the bigger picture. This is important for several reasons:

- It will help with the career decisions you will inevitably have to make (e.g. deciding between two job options). It is much easier to make difficult choices if you are clear on your long-term goals.
- It will help you identify the skills you need to acquire or the actions you need to take to make your future aspirations a reality.
- Having a clear idea of where you are heading will give you additional drive to keep going towards your ultimate aim.

Setting interim and long-term goals is what helps create momentum and is something that so few of us do as a matter of course. If you are really considering what you want out of life, looking ahead is vital, and we think these exercises are some of the most important in the book to help create your forward momentum. Without goals, you will find that your days, weeks, months and years get filled up with 'stuff' that aids day-to-day living but, when you look back, leaves you wondering why you never really achieved what you had intended.

While here we are principally concerned with your career aspirations, goals in other parts of your life are important too, so make sure they are compatible with each other.

Chris was working in India and he used this exercise to sit down with his wife to jointly think about what they wanted from life in the next five, ten, fifteen years; they also took into account the ages of their children – anticipating a time when they wouldn't have dependents. Chris considered all his options against the outputs from all his self-assessment exercises to help him decide which was the best career path to go down. Options on the table included taking another managing director role in another company, moving into a different industry, or pursuing with the company he founded and had a shareholding in. After researching the options and scoring them against his criteria, he decided to pursue the entrepreneurial path. You can listen to his full story at at http://thecareerfarm.com/mde10/

Long-term goals exercise

When completing the exercise below, we strongly suggest you consider all areas of your life such as career (or work), relationships, recreational interests, personal growth, material goals and social goals. It is useful to realize how these goals interrelate and which ones are dependent on others, as this can affect the overall picture you build of your ideal life.

It is interesting to take a look at where you hope/expect to be in the future. This is not about writing your future in stone, it is about thinking through what you want to achieve for yourself and for those who are important to you. It helps if you do this review regularly so you can assess whether your goals need to be adjusted or changed; by looking at various key stages through your life, you may gain some perspective about what you are actually looking for and perhaps start thinking earlier how you are going to attain it.

For this exercise, we would like you to draw a circle on five pieces of paper and divide the circle into six pieces labelled as in Figure 2.5.

At the head of the first piece of paper write the date and your age.

In each of the sections, write down what score you would give that aspect of your life out of 10. Next, answer the questions for each section and write down one thing you could do that would improve that score by just one.

Is your life, according to each score out of 10 and the answers you have given, a balanced one? Is that what you are aiming for?

On the second piece of paper, write down your age five years from now. Answer the questions and write down one thing you could do to improve each aspect of your life if you pushed yourself.

On the third piece of paper, write down your age in ten years' time and follow the process above. On the fourth page, write down your age in twenty years' time and finally, on the fifth piece, your age in thirty years' time. Answer all the questions as you go, in as much detail as you can. If there's not enough room in the box, transfer your answers to a new piece of paper – the more detail you put down the better.

If you struggle to answer the final question about how to stretch your goals, you can leave this question blank for each section other than the first. Some people find it helpful to stretch their thinking for the future and others find it a step too far – it's a matter of finding what works for you.

Now, when you review those five pages, how do you feel? Is that the life you've dreamed of? If not, what would you change? What would you improve? How have you stretched yourself?

Keep revising the pages until you have created a view of your life as you would want it to be.

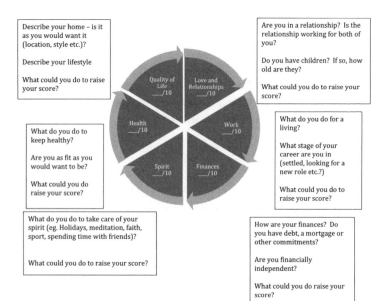

Figure 2.5

Case study: Sarah Marsh

In my last year at school I really wanted to be a graphic designer but my parents thought that jobs in art were for people who dropped out. I was good at maths so I was persuaded to train as an accountant, which I soon realized did not need me to be good at maths! Unhappy with this career I 'dropped' into sales with a health insurer. I quite enjoyed this for about ten years, and was good at it, but I felt limited, as if there had to be more to life. I wanted to do something that made more of a difference, that I enjoyed and could motivate and help people. I had always liked health and fitness so trained as a personal trainer, which I enjoyed, but this was not a respected or well-paid job and I realized I had rushed the decision without thinking about longevity of the role, prospects, etc.

I started to consider if I could retrain further still in the medical/ health field, but did not know where to start. This was when a friend suggested I work with a career coach. At the same time I had some difficult decisions to make personally; my husband and I needed to embark upon IVF if we were to try for a family. I felt stuck and was going round in circles … I thought that if I was successful in starting a family I couldn't retrain – my life would be too full with caring for my child/family – and that if I didn't get pregnant could I be something different? This was where my coach was fantastic. She asked me to do two five-year plans: one with a family at the end, one without – and guess what? The result was the same. This made me feel really sure that I did want to retrain, so with help from my coach I 'tried on' various different roles: doctor, physiotherapist, osteopath. Looking back now this seems relatively easy, but it took lots and lots of research, and it needed me to look at how practically I would achieve this – costs/ time involved, that sort of thing. I decided I wanted to retrain as a physiotherapist. I would be working in the medical/health field, while on a personal level my nan had had a stroke and had received no physiotherapy – so it seemed completely the right solution. My coach helped me along the journey; she didn't do things for me, but questioned and encouraged me, helping when I felt I couldn't make it. So four-and-a-half years later I have qualified as a physiotherapist, discovered a love of yoga, completed teacher training and now combine yoga and physiotherapy for my patients.

I love my new career; I would recommend coaching to anyone. It opens your mind to options you would never have considered;

it takes time, but it's realistic, considering your commitments but helping you see there are new opportunities out there for us all.

If you don't feel that this exercise has truly captured your future, here are a couple of others that we give to clients to help them as they develop their vision for their lives to come.

Your success article

If you are someone to whom writing comes easily, then this exercise could be the one for you.

- You are going to write an article as if you are the new successful you, comfortably settled in your new dream role.
- Which publication would you like a success profile to appear in?
- What is that publication's style of writing – what would they focus the article on?
- Now write the article describing how you started on your career and the steps that have been important to you to achieve success. Focus on the key stages and what it feels like to have achieved your aims; write about what you have learned that you will draw on in the future.

Your life collage

This exercise can be very useful for people who enjoy being creative (it doesn't matter whether you think you are good at being creative!).

- Get a large piece of paper (preferably A0 which you can buy at most stationers) which will roll relatively easily – as you will want to store for future reference. You will also need as large a pile of magazines as possible, scissors, glue, coloured pens and a large surface to work on, combined with some time to yourself.
- Flick through the magazines and rip out any pictures, words, statements, colours, etc. that you are attracted to. At this stage, don't spend too much time wondering why you are attracted them – the more images you can gather the better.
- Once you have a large quantity of images to choose from, start to sort them into piles. You are looking for images and words that you would like to see in your 'perfect' life. This is time to play and not become too serious. Enjoy yourself. Look at each image you have ripped out – what was it about it that attracted you? What does it represent? Is there a better image to represent that feeling, situation or person? So if you want to live by the sea, is there an image to represent that? If you want to earn huge amounts of money, how are you going to show that? What about your hobbies? What about the people you want to have around you? Are there photos of family and friends or is there a picture to symbolize the relationships you'd like to have?
- Now start to add the pictures to the large piece of paper. You can add words, colours, anything that you feel will add to the image of what you are aiming for. Once your collage

is completed, have you added any pictures that give you clues to your future career direction?

Julie was still stuck about her future career direction having completed all the exercises, so she made a life collage. She was working in the City and had been on a steady promotion track in financial services. Her family was proud of her as she was the first person in the family to have been to university and to have the kind of financial success she was enjoying. Julie, on the other hand, was depressed, angry and unsatisfied but didn't know how to change that. We were both surprised to see that her collage included no pictures of a business woman, money or promotion. Instead, there were pictures of beaches, children, learning, among others. That was the starting point of our brainstorming. What became clear was that she was in her career so as not to disappoint her family and not for herself. After much discussion, she decided to leave and retrain as a school teacher. She is very happy with the move and is now working at a school where the playground faces a beach!

Chapter 18

Putting this all together – evaluating options

> Great things are done by a series of small things brought together.
>
> *Vincent van Gogh*

Now you have completed the self-assessment exercises, it's time to bring everything together. The most effective way we have found to do that and have all the information readily available in one place is by using the matrix on page 126. We have provided an example of a partially completed matrix on page 125.

Your aim here is to combine into the matrix all of the components gathered from the assessment exercises that will comprise your perfect job. At this stage, don't exclude things that you just don't think are possible. You might like to use a spreadsheet for your matrix – there is one available to download at www.howtotakechargeofyourcareer.com

In the matrix:

1   Choose criteria from your assessment exercises that you believe to be important in your future career. For some people it might be using their top skills, so all the skills are put in the grid. Others may decide that they only want to consider one of their interests when evaluating career options, so only one would be listed.

2   Look at your needs and make sure you cover the things

that are important to you (e.g. the salary range you
want to earn, your ideal location, etc.).

3   Add in other preferences (such as type of environment
and type of boss) if these are important to you.

There is no maximum number of items to put across the
top of the matrix, so don't feel constrained, although we do
encourage people to try and come up with at least twenty-five
items that would be components of their dream job, with the
average being about fifty different items.

Once you have filled in all the criteria that will make up your
ideal job, in the 'jobs' column, list the last couple of jobs (or
main jobs) you have held and then tick off how many criteria
they meet in total. This gives you a review of how suitable
those previous jobs have been and a benchmark against
which to compare other possible options. The results can
often be enlightening! For example, if you know that your
previous job, which was fine but not great, gave you a score of
11 out of 25, you are definitely seeking more than a score
of 11 for the roles you are contemplating.

At this stage, you may also want to highlight the criteria
that are non-negotiable as far as you are concerned – these
might include salary and location – as there is no point in
researching jobs that will ultimately not meet your needs.
You may also want to weight some criteria higher than others
as they are more important to you.

If you don't know whether a job or sector meets your criteria,
instead of adding a tick or a cross, put in a question mark to
remind you to find out the information when you come to
researching at a later date.

Possible Jobs	Value: People Orientated	Value: Time with Family	Value: Adventure	Skills: Entrepreneurial	Skills: Leadership	Skills: Strategic Planning	Interest: Wine	Salary: £50k to £80k	Location: London	Boss Must Give Me Autonomy	TOTAL TICKS
Management Consultant in a Small Niche Firm	✓	?	x	x	✓	✓	x	✓	✓	?	5
Management Consultant in Large Firm	✓	x	x	x	x	✓	x	✓	✓	?	4
Analyst	?	x	x	x	x	?	x	✓	✓	?	2
Set up Online Wine Shop	✓	?	✓	✓	✓	✓	✓	?	✓	✓	8

Figure 2.6

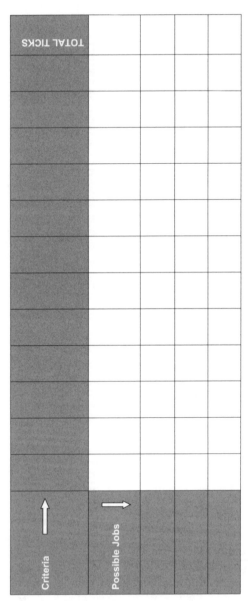

Figure 2.7

Chapter 19

Brainstorming options

> An idea that is not dangerous is unworthy of being called an idea at all.
>
> *Oscar Wilde*

The final stage of Part II is the one that career changers often find the most daunting: brainstorming options for possible jobs. They often say that their brains have gone completely blank and if they *can* come up with ideas, they dismiss them out of hand before trying them out on the matrix.

Another common question here is: 'what if I just don't know that a job exists so I narrow things down too quickly?' At some point, you are going to have to draw a line in the sand and start researching what you have come up with so far rather than prevaricating and wondering about what you don't know. Once you have decided on a sector or role, you will start the research, which may well lead you to those afore-mentioned 'hidden' roles, so concentrate on what you know rather than what you don't.

Tom was keen to move into the wine trade but was unsure about the direction and had initially come up with a list of three potential roles that he could consider. One of his pieces of research to gather more 'insider language' about the industry was to find out about as many jobs in the wine trade as he could. By the time he had finished, he had come up with eighty-seven different jobs – fourteen of which were distinct possibilities and two of which, when put onto the grid, were worth pursuing with more energy. He then began working in the wine trade as a buyer.

Thinking laterally

This is your chance to play with ideas so don't rule anything out at this stage. If you get stuck, think as laterally as you can.

> Mike had a background in the financial services industry and was keen to move out. One of his key interests was the theatre. He started investigating whether it was possible to bring the two worlds together by finding business angels and investors for film and theatre productions.

If you are finding it hard to come up with ideas, ask friends and family to look at the list of criteria and see whether they can help. Even if they are 'outside the box', their comments may spark an idea. Once you have come up with as many ideas as possible, you will see that there are perhaps three or four possibilities that either have ticked more of the criteria than any others OR that keep piquing your interest and you want to know more.

You should now be in a position to decide which career(s) to start investigating first. We will cover how to go about this next stage in Part III.

You may well find the matrix useful to refer back to in the future especially if you ever have to evaluate two options (perhaps two job offers). Looking again at your criteria for the perfect job may make the decision somewhat easier and help you to consider your long-term goals and what positions would work well for you for the longer term. For some, this has meant taking a salary cut or a seemingly sideways move to gain experience to move forward.

Case study: Jamie Lumley

After finishing a degree in Geography I had no idea what I wanted to do for a career. I took a temporary position as an admin assistant for the NHS as an interim step. I ended up staying there for a year but I was very bored and I came to realize that working in an office was not for me. But I didn't really know what I did want to do, other than hopefully working outdoors.

I went through the various exercises and started to get a clearer view on what I wanted; we brainstormed until I came up with a list of careers I might possibly be interested in. After some more research, it emerged that tree surgery seemed to tick all the boxes of things that I was looking for in a job. I started a part-time course in arboriculture while working as a gardener. After the course I got my chainsaw and climbing certificates and found a job with a tree surgery company. I started off working as a groundsman, getting some occasional practice at climbing. Now I am a second climber, working up to becoming a full time climber.

The biggest challenge I faced in starting off in tree surgery was being unsure whether or not I could cope with the physical aspect of the job. Getting on the job experience was very important to persuade me that I was capable of taking on the job – I wouldn't have wanted to have wasted my time and energy without knowing that. So my advice to anyone wanting to get into tree surgery or any career involving retraining would be to get some work experience before investing in college courses etc. I have just finished a more advanced arboriculture course. I love the work and definitely feel I have found the right career for me. I plan to work as a tree surgeon for another five years or so, after which I will become a tree officer or arboriculture consultant.

It is very easy at this stage to narrow down your options too quickly and often this is because of preconceived ideas or incomplete knowledge. Ask yourself if you are dismissing an option because you know it will not work for you or because you don't have enough information to make an informed decision. Perhaps through your investigation you will find that the job you have originally identified is not for you but that, through your research, you have found an associated job that is absolutely perfect and ticks most of your criteria.

Chapter 20

Optional extras – psychometric and career tests

> Knowing is not enough; we must apply. Willing is not enough; we must do.
>
> *Johann Wolfgang von Goethe*

One area we have not covered so far is alternative ways of gathering information that may help in your decision-making process. If you have completed the exercises we have described and still feel you would like additional data, you may want to consider adding this extra information into the mix. Also, because most of the previous exercises rely on you analysing your experience, this section may be useful for people with little work experience to draw on.

We often get asked whether it is useful to take some of the career-focused psychometric tests to give additional insights. Our answer may not be the one you want to hear (most people want a definitive yes or no!) – it is up to you! Working on your career and deciding your career path can be hard work and many clients hope that personality questionnaires and ability tests hold the answer. While they are useful tools to help you start analysing yourself or generating ideas, they are not necessarily an end in themselves. However, for those with little experience to analyse, such as school leavers and graduates, psychometric tests can be a useful first step and provide a framework to work within. If you have taken a test which has resonated with you, then by all means factor it into the information you are gathering. If you feel additional insight from a different direction would help with your thinking, we have outlined below some of the options available on the market. Sadly, there is no 'crystal ball' and no one knows you better than you. It takes hard work and persistence to work on your career but it's worth it – you're worth it!

Over the years we have worked with many occupational psychologists to administer these tests for clients. Emma Greggains, a highly experienced psychologist who has worked extensively with clients in both the private and public sectors, gave us her view on using psychometric tests in the career development process.

Where to find psychometric tests

There is an ever-increasing choice of psychometric tests available to support career development, many of them offered free on the internet. While many tests can be useful for generating ideas or looking at a specific ability or person-ality trait, deciding which tests are likely to be helpful for you can be a time-consuming and confusing exercise.

We strongly recommend that if you are interested in taking one or more psychometric tests, you enlist the advice and help of a professional who has been trained in the various tests available and can interpret the results; they will be able to advise which (if any) tests will add value to your career development journey. The British Psychological Society (BPS) has introduced a system of accreditation to support best practice in test use. Practitioners will hold either a 'Level A' Certificate of Competence in Occupational

Testing, or the more advanced 'Level B' Certificate depending on the type of test being administered. The website www.psychtesting.org.uk/directories is a register held by the BPS. There is also an International Testing Commission at www.intestcom.org which facilitates information about test use between countries. However, it does not hold a register of international test users. Specific standards and a register of test users will be provided by each country's own equivalent of the BPS (e.g. the American Psychological Association).

The main reason why you might want to consider using psychometric test findings in your career development process is primarily to raise self-awareness and stimulate discussion. A skilled practitioner will facilitate your test feedback session by drawing on various sources of information, such as your existing skill set, your behavioural preferences and ability test results. A cautionary note, however: a test feedback session is only a springboard for exploring different career options and should not become a distraction from the real task at hand!

Choosing the right test for you

A few words about what characterizes a test that you can have confidence in. First, is it reliable? In other words, are the scores produced consistent over time? And secondly, is it valid? Does the test actually measure what it says it does? Robust tests that have been rigorously researched and developed will always be supported by reliability and validity data. The British Psychological Society's Psychological Testing Centre (PTC) (www.psychtesting.org.uk) provides a useful source of information about the services relating to standards in tests.

It is useful to think about psychometric tests as either tests of **maximum performance** (such as those that measure ability or aptitude) or tests of **typical performance** (such as those that measure personality, values or interests). Each has its place in adding value to the career development process.

Tests of maximum performance

These include aptitude and ability tests and are designed to measure an individual's potential to learn. Ability test results need to be interpreted by a practitioner who holds a 'Level A' Certificate of Competence in Occupational Testing. Many ability tests developed by the well-known test publishers are available online as well as in pencil and paper versions for ease of administration. Ability tests tend to have questions for which there is usually a right or wrong answer and a time limit.

There is a wide range of psychometrics that test how much ability individuals have in particular domains, such as abstract reasoning, numerical reasoning or verbal reasoning. Aptitude tests are also available that are specifically job-related; for example, tests that measure aptitude for computer programming or proof reading. In practical terms, ability tests are extremely useful for identifying what you are good at. For example, a high score on a test of numerical reasoning may open up your thinking to a wide range of different career options.

Tests of typical performance

These tend to be self-report questionnaires and broadly fall into three categories. The majority of these questionnaires will require interpretation by a practitioner who holds a

'Level B' Certificate of Competence in Occupational Testing and has been trained in the specific tool being used.

- **Personality questionnaires** assess typical or preferred ways of thinking or behaving. These do not have right or wrong answers and will usually attempt to assess how much an individual has of a particular *trait*, such as extroversion or perfectionism. By building up a profile of an individual's preference for behaving in certain ways, it is possible to identify career options that may (or may not) 'fit' their personality. For example, what does my preference for working in a quiet environment with opportunities to analyse people's behaviour mean for carrying out a new job role?

Numerous personality questionnaires are currently available and it is not the object of this review to list them all. However, the most robust tools are likely to be produced by the major test publishers because they have the resources to focus on extensive research and development. Usually, there is no time limit when taking a personality questionnaire.

- **Values and motivation questionnaires** are useful for assessing what is important to an individual. What drives you and what do your personal values look like? For instance, one person may report that they are motivated by a need for affiliation with other people while another may strongly value a role that offers material reward.

There is a comprehensive selection of well-validated values and motivation questionnaires currently available on the market. Again, you will need to enlist the support of a 'Level B' accredited practitioner with appropriate training when using one of these questionnaires as part of your career development process.

It is worth mentioning one of the most widely known bespoke career development tools, 'Career Anchors', in this section. 'Career Anchors' was developed by Edgar Schein, a leader in the field of career and professional studies, and is designed to help you think about what you really want out of a career. He used the term 'career anchors' to describe 'patterns of self-perceived talents, motives and values' which 'guide, constrain, stabilize and integrate the person's career'.

• **Interest inventories** assess people's preferences for particular activities. An occupational interest questionnaire will provide data about an individual's preference for working in a particular type of job, such as nursing or engineering.

There are limited well-validated interest inventories currently available. Training is provided for certain tools, but unlike with personality and motivation questionnaires, most interest inventories do not require users to have 'Level B' accreditation. Possibly the most widely known is the 'Strong Interest Inventory' which is based on Holland's six general occupational themes. 'Strong' has been used extensively for many years as part of the self-assessment stage of career planning.

As stated in the introduction to this section, if you feel that you need additional information to facilitate your career development review, well-chosen psychometric tests can provide you with objective and targeted data. For example, just because you are good at something does not necessarily mean that you are interested in pursuing it as part of your career! You may score highly on a numerical reasoning test but self-report feedback from an occupational personality profile shows that compared to others you are less likely to enjoy analysing data in your job. This type of feedback is extremely useful in the career development discussion and may result in one of those 'lightbulb' moments that can change the focus of your thinking.

Summary sheet

Now you have gathered all of the information that will prove useful in your job search, in addition to the matrix, it is useful to have a summary sheet that you can keep with you to refer to constantly when searching for job opportunities online, explaining what you are looking for when talking to a new contact, or to keep adding to as your thinking becomes ever clearer. Whether you store this on paper or on your phone, we recommend you keep it easily to hand.

My transferable skills:	My key achievements:
What I value:	My interests:
What I look for in a workplace:	What I look for in colleagues and managers:

My unique selling points	What three words do I want people to think about me?
My long-term aspirations:	What I am working on to develop (e.g. skills, experience, behaviour)
The sectors/functions I am researching:	Who would I like to meet or be introduced to?
My action plan this month:	

Part III: Now what? How to research, brainstorm and move forward

> Knowledge is power.
>
> *Sir Francis Bacon*

If you've ever read this style of book before, you may well have seen the author exhorting you to go through each stage one at a time and to follow the process from beginning to end. Over the years, we have both read countless of these books for our own development, research and interest. We have done what the majority of people do: flick through the book and think, I'll get back to doing the exercises when I get a moment. It was only when we started putting this book together that we suddenly understood the pleas of those other authors. We know, through years of practice, that this methodology can really work if you just go through each phase systematically. If we were with you in person, coaching you through this process, we would be there to spot those moments of doubt written on your face or to deal with the 'yes buts...' that inevitably follow. We hope that you will be determined enough to do this for yourself. If you have sidetracked the exercises so far or have missed out one or two that you don't feel you want to do, you should go back now and complete them – starting this new section with a renewed vigour and belief that you really can work towards your career goal.

If we are not giving you the benefit of the doubt and you have followed the book – we apologise! If you have completed Part II, you will now have a sense of your key skills and experience, will have a good idea of what you are looking for in your ideal job, and will have brainstormed some ideas of careers to research. We also hope you have overcome any obstacles that are standing in your path or have a plan for how to cope with them when or if they appear.

Part III covers how you narrow down your brainstormed ideas into tangible options. We will look at how you deal with the world of work when it doesn't seem to fit with your life circumstances, either in the short or long term, and how to create an action plan. Finally, in Part IV, we will review best practice in the art of job applications and negotiation.

The start to this section can appear daunting to some as most of the work to date can be done below the radar – you can look at yourself and potential options without necessarily sharing what you are doing with other people. Now you will have to venture out into the open and that can be a nerve-wracking time for many, especially those who are naturally introverted. Now, more than ever, having a positive support network around you who will spur you on can help enormously. You may occasionally find your heart in your mouth as you make some research calls or start networking. Given that the research piece is a crucial element of the process and incredibly useful, we hope you will work your way through any residual fear with the end goal of finding the right job clearly in your sights.

Chapter 21

Researching – separating perception from reality

As we have mentioned several times in the book so far, the more real information/data you have, the easier it is going to be to make a decision about whether a career or company is the right one for you. We so often lose sight of what is reality and what is perception, so systematic research from a variety of different sources will help immeasurably as you start to narrow down your brainstormed options to a clear favourite where you can apply all your energies.

For many clients this stage takes months. The length of this phase is driven by whether you are already working or not and how much time you can dedicate to it.

Finding time for research

How long it will take you will depend on the priority you assign to your research and the clear, measurable goals you have set in this area. As we know, occasionally life can get in the way of the best-laid plans. We know from experience that it is very easy to let this phase drift and you can lose track of what you are trying to find out and why. The more time you can make in your already busy life, the faster you will complete this part of the process. We know that if you have a full-time job or children, time will be at a premium, but time you devote to this process will be useful – even the odd snatched five minutes of research on the internet still gets you closer to your goal. Many people want to move through this phase as quickly as possible, with the end goal of knowing where they're heading so tantalizingly close, but the time you spend doing this research in depth will pay dividends in the long run. Go at the right pace for you – just maintain momentum and do little and often rather than putting it to one side and swearing to yourself that you'll get back to it sometime. Sometime rarely comes ...

Maintaining your career folder

As you go through this research stage, it is very important to review your matrix. It is your touchstone – after every piece of research you will need to 'check in' and evaluate what you have found alongside what you have identified as important to you and what you want to achieve. Some options will be ceremoniously struck off the list. This is a positive step as you can then focus more of your time and energy on the other areas you want to investigate that are still viable options. As you gather information from your research, add it to your career folder so that you know where everything is rather than having to start from scratch each time. For example, if you are on the internet and see a press release from a company in the sector you are potentially interested in but are running out the door for an appointment, save it, put it in your career folder and read it when you have a moment. Sod's Law says that if you think you'll find the site and article again when you get back, you will either forget all about it or won't be able to find it. Also, if you keep all the information in one place, when you have a meeting with someone from the sector or company, you can easily find all the references you have come across to review before the meeting, saving time. So whether you go for a physical file or an online tool like www.evernote.com (one of several electronic filing systems available), keeping everything together will definitely make your life easier in the long run. Your matrix is your starting point to highlighting what information you need to know – whether it's about the sector you would like to investigate, the function you would like to know more about, or to answer more specific questions to ascertain whether, for example, a potential career will pay you the salary you are looking for or will match up with a particular value or skill you have identified as important.

Once you have clarified the information you need, the next stage is to work out how best to find that information. Your starting point is the internet, which is a great resource for gathering information. Think of every possible route to find out what you are looking for and follow each link to a new site, until you feel you have exhausted all your options. If you do not have access to a computer, try your local library. They will usually have computers you can access and they also often stock copies of periodicals from major industry sectors which may give you new information. Once you have gathered all the data you can from these sources, you will be left with a list of information you need that can best be obtained from people who work in that field.

Trends

Of course no one knows what the future may bring, but we encourage you to take a look at anticipated future trends and what it might mean for your career path. After all, surely it's better to move into a growing industry than one in decline? We would encourage you to add this into the research component of your job search so you can consider where you might need to retrain or improve your skills. There are various reports you can read – for example, the World Economic Forum publishes various reports, including one on the Future of Jobs. Keep an eye out for new sectors that are gathering momentum such as FinTech or EdTech. Perhaps logistics via drone delivery.

Once you have found a sector that is of interest, ask those who you are interviewing where they see it developing in the future and which aspects of the sector will die away. You might of course be thinking about setting up your own business and part of seeing a gap in the market is about also recognizing trends. Some very successful companies have seen a new opportunity and capitalized on it. Sometimes this is more by luck than design as occasionally success can be attributed to timing. Certainly considering the effect of future trends should be part of the decision-making process if you are starting a business. And at the very least, if you decide to go down the traditional route of finding investors, you will need to include future trends in your business plan. So consider: does your business idea follow a perceived gap in the market? Build on it? Or is set to capitalize on a completely new trend?

Another place you can gain insight into the future is at conferences. We encourage you to research what conferences are happening in your field. This is useful for two reasons: 1) you can investigate what subjects are being presented as often these will be topics that are future orientated or are important issues in the industry, giving you a clue as to where there might be an opportunity; and 2) you can see which companies are exhibiting and/or speakers are presenting, giving you a ready-made list of target companies and potential contacts. Ideally you should attend some of these conferences as face-to-face contact is invaluable for networking, but sometimes the cost can be prohibitive. Luckily, for most conferences a lot of useful information can be gleaned online.

Different types of research

Passive information gathering

This is probably the most obvious form of research, but worth mentioning all the same. So far, you have a list of potential sectors or even potential roles that you might be interested in. If it is a sector or job you are already familiar with, you will be supplementing the information you already have. If, however, these are completely new sectors to you, then you are about to go on a fascinating voyage of discovery into a new world. OK, perhaps that's a little grand ... but before you get started on the research, you need to be in the right frame of mind to hunt out all the vital detail you need to make a very important decision – one that might affect a good deal of your happiness and sense of fulfilment in the workplace (no pressure!).

Over the years, we have found that many of our clients have tried to cut short this part and feel that a cursory look at a sector will tell them all they need to know. This may well stand you in good stead to make primary decisions based on factors such as the career will not pay you the salary you need or will require high fitness levels which is not you at all. However, if a sector or career starts to look like it might well be a possibility, the more in-depth information you gather, the better off you will be. This is for a few reasons:

1   It will allow you to make an informed decision on whether it matches with what you are looking for.

2   You will start to get a greater insight into the industry.
3   You will start to inadvertently gather 'insider language' which will help in future information gathering with individuals involved in the industry and enable you to come across more impressively at interviews.
4   You may be surprised! Your initial impression may be outdated or may only affect one part of a sector, so the more you know, the better informed you will be to make a decision and to ensure the information is correct.

'Insider language'

If you think of anything you have a certain amount of knowledge about (your favourite musician, hobby, club, city), you will recognize that there are certain words and phrases that only someone who is similarly knowledgeable will know. You may recall being at a social engagement where there's lots of noise; you are deep in conversation with someone but then you hear someone else in a different group – a group you haven't been listening to – mention something that resonates with you, like the name of an obscure artist whose show you have just seen. We instantly look for similarity in people and that sort of reference gives us an immediate connection. We recognize someone who is probably like-minded ... an insider. On the other hand, we've all come across people who have ended up looking foolish when they pretend to be what they're not and dig themselves into a hole. The same is true when you express an interest in a sector or career. The more information you have or the more 'insider language' you hear, assimilate and start using naturally, the more likely you are to be accepted as one of the 'in-crowd' and you'll have created a bond. As with all of us, we are more likely to be well disposed and helpful to those who are on the same wavelength as us or who talk the same language. So the upshot of all that is that the more information you uncover, however insignificant it might seem, the better – it may just give you the edge in future conversations with people who are able to help you in the job search. And anything that can you give an edge is worth having!

General information

The starting point (if you don't already have it) is generalist sector information. This is the foundation to any future research and may well give you vital details that can count as an option from your matrix.

Questions to consider include:

- How broad is the sector – are there different aspects to it?
- Which are the main organizations in that sector?
- How is the sector doing in the economic climate – is it on the rise or in decline?
- Have any books been written about the sector as a whole?
- What are the main periodicals written for that sector and how can you access them?
- Does the sector hold conferences that are open to the public – if so, where and when?
- Who are the main commentators on the sector (journalists, experts, etc.)?
- Is there a governing body for the sector?

Again, the internet is a great place to start with this kind of research. First, put the sector into a search engine and see what comes up – is it a company name? Does it have a Wikipedia entry? Once you have exhausted the information from this preliminary search, work through each of the questions above using the search engine. Make a note of key Internet sites that are useful or names that keep coming up that may be useful as you progress. As you work through this research, ask yourself whether it is making things any clearer for you. It may seem obvious, but it is easy to get caught up in gathering information and then losing sight of why you're gathering it. Are you starting to see a particular part of the sector that is appealing more than any other? What is it about that part of the sector that is interesting you? Is this sector still looking like a good option for you? If you don't know the answer, what else do you need to know about the sector to decide whether it is a good option? Keep going until you have a sense of whether the sector is the one for you.

Once you have enough information to decide whether, say, the financial services sector appeals to you, can you narrow the sector down further into a specific area of the financial services sector? If, in your research, you have decided that private banking is the place you would like to orientate your search further, you can then refine the search for further information. You may find that you still have more than one sector that has piqued your interest, so try and narrow each sector down to one particular area of focus with the information you have gathered.

More detailed information

Look at what you have already gathered on the particular area that you are now going to focus on. What information do you still need? To get you started, here are some ideas for gathering more detailed information:

1   Put together a list of all the roles you can find in the industry you are interested in – make the list as

exhaustive as possible (remember Tom who managed to come up with eighty-seven options in the wine trade?).

2   Delete any of these roles that do not appeal at all.
3   Find out what qualifications or entry requirements are needed for each of the roles.
4   Who are the main employers in this industry – does their website have additional information that would prove useful? Do they advertise potential roles on their website?
5   Gather more detailed information from magazines or trade association websites, paying particular attention to any articles that draw your eye – what aspects of these articles interested you? Could that give you additional information or suggest this is an avenue to investigate further?
6   Start putting together a list of key protagonists in the industry – are there industry lecturers, journalists, people who are key to the industry who have been profiled? Can you get information on how to get in touch with those people either by phone or by email?

As you gather more information, some of it will lead you to want to develop new lines of investigation and some will make it clear that a direction is not for you. Each time that you add a new line of enquiry or shut one down, it is progress, even if it doesn't always feel that way.

Since childhood, Caroline had always had an interest in accident investigation but when she had mentioned that to her family, they had joked with her about it, telling her it was far too gruesome a profession for her. She had taken that at face value and so had never pursued it as a possible career. When she started her coaching, she talked about how she was still intrigued about accident investigation and kept coming back to it as an option. Her first piece of research was to find out all the different kinds of accident investigation and entry requirements. She discovered that you needed to go through the police service to train in accident investigation so arranged a meeting at the local recruitment centre to discuss how she might get into the field. They were extremely helpful – they told her that she would need to train as a police officer and then, after a certain amount of time, she could apply to train in accident investigation but that there were no guarantees. She spoke to a couple of people in the field and did a little further investigation, but what became clear was that she was not interested in a career with the police without a guarantee that she would end up in the discipline of her choice. Her research also gave her enough information for her to realize that the career was not for her – not because it was too gruesome, but for family circumstances. As soon as she had shut this down as a possibility, she was able to focus more on what felt right for her. She is now in her chosen field of sales and marketing.

Often we find our clients have to cross things off the list in order to move forward. This act of finally dismissing a career avenue can be tremendously liberating, so that option that had been floating around in your head can either move to being a serious contender for your future career or removed as an option once and for all. Return to the matrix. Has the information you have gathered so far answered any of the question marks you had in place? Have you deleted any of your brainstorm options because of your research? Have you added any new options to the matrix and marked it up against your criteria?

Active information gathering: Networking

As you will see from Caroline's story, once she had done all the information gathering she could from passive sources, the next step was to start talking to people working in the field she wanted to know more about.

When networking is mentioned, it usually conjures up images of rooms full of people you don't know who you have to approach to get their contact details or to give them yours – a hugely stressful thought for most people, even some extroverts! We help people we know, like and trust and that is your jumping off point. It is so easy to overlook the people closest to you as a source of help and assistance: it is very important you tell your friends and family that you are researching certain jobs or fields. It is highly likely you don't know all their network and you certainly don't know who they are going to sit next to on a train or talk to at a party – they need to be your eyes and ears. Many people have someone in the family or a friend who is always sending newspaper clippings or chatting to anyone and everyone – recruit them to your exploration team.

Now it's your turn to start your networking and gathering information from the people who are in the know. There's no getting away from it – this is the part that most people find the most daunting. Picking up the phone to talk to someone to ask for help can be nerve-wracking, particularly if you don't know them or the link to them is tenuous at best. However, at this stage, it's a crucial part of the process, as you are still likely to have many questions about what is required for a particular position in the industry of your choice. We have worked with hundreds of people who have faced this stage with trepidation, so we have tried to lay out some tried and tested routes to getting the information you need in as painless a way as possible. Clearly, adapt these thoughts so that they work for you and the person you are approaching – but they should give you a good starting point.

First steps

As you have been gathering your information, hopefully you will have started to list some names of key individuals who might be useful for you to meet. Do you have their contact information? If not, that's the next step. If you know where they work, perhaps the company's website can give you their contact information or, at the least, a main switchboard number. We will return to this group of individuals in due course, but making a 'cold call' – i.e. a call to someone who you don't know and who has no reason to take your call – can be the most scary. So let's look at how you can gather some 'warmer' options: those people where there might be some form of connection in place already.

You may have heard of the concept of 'six degrees of separation'. It was an idea that was developed in a play, and later a film, written by John Guare, that suggests that if you are one link away from each person you know, and then two links away from each person that each of those individuals know and so on, there comes a point where each of us is only six links away from every individual on earth. There are several networking sites that work on that basis – our favourite for business networking being LinkedIn (www.linkedin.com) which can help you connect through your network to someone else.

You may shrug your shoulders and say that it won't work for

you, but we think you'll be surprised if you approach this portion of research with an open mind.

Your first step is to start telling those people who are one link away from you that you are trying to meet people who are involved in a particular job or industry and ask if they know anyone they could introduce you to. Start with the easy ones – your family and closest friends – but then you can gradually widen the people you ask. You will be surprised at the contacts people manage to come up with – and don't discount asking anyone. Your cousin the farmer may not be the most obvious person to ask if they know anyone in sport management, but perhaps they were at school with someone whose partner works in the field. Never presume you know who can help – ask!

One of the things to keep in mind as you do this is that people love to help, especially if it makes them seem knowledgeable or an expert in the process! If one of your family or friends approached you to help find individuals in your chosen field, would you offer to help? We are hoping you would! Work on the basis that the people you are going to approach feel the same way.

Case study: Kaye Kent

My best subject has always been art. However, there wasn't very good career advice available at my school and I ended up drifting into art college and then a History of Art degree. Still unsure what I wanted to do after graduating, I went on to complete a Heritage Studies MA, to train as a curator. After getting my first professional job in a gallery on the south coast, I realized working in the public sector wasn't for me, so I tried various jobs in commercial galleries, which suited me better. However, I always had to go where the work was and ended up moving to new places around the country several times. I finally got my big break working as an art consultant for a company in Liverpool – and it really was my dream job! I had to create a range of art from scratch to suit interior design projects, which involved travelling all over the UK, looking at art and meeting artists. Heaven! The problem was, I had found a job I loved, but it was located in the wrong place as I desperately wanted to move back home to Yorkshire. Finally, push came to shove and I decided for the first time to put my personal life before work, so I took the plunge and relocated. I tried to continue with my job from home for a while, but I felt very isolated and missed being in a busy working environment. With so few other opportunities around, I realized a career change was my only option.

I had always been interested in the idea of working in TV, but had no idea where to start. It was through a friend who is a cameraman that I was advised to try and get some work experience at Yorkshire TV. I was accepted on a two-week placement in the art department, during which I got my first insight into this world. With luck, a new period drama was going into production as my placement finished, and I was taken on as the art department runner – which was a great opportunity to work on an actual production. Since then, I have worked on several films and TV drama programmes, and am now working as a production buyer/ set decorator. This role ties in with the knowledge of period styles I gained through training as a curator, and I can use skills from my art consulting career such as working to design briefs and sourcing appropriate dressing for various sets. Every job is different, which always keeps my working life varied and challenging. The hours are long, and the lack of job security as a freelancer can be stressful, but I have finally found a vocation which brings together my creative strengths and knowledge and I am so happy I had the courage to make a change.

Top tips

If someone gives you a lead, follow it up – there's nothing worse than helping someone out who does nothing about it. Thank them for their help and then let them know how the contact has worked out – we have found that the vast majority of people like to help but they also like to be thanked!

If they do have a lead that you can follow up, ask if they would be prepared to make the introduction rather than just giving you the contact details. If they are willing, ask if they would find out if the person they are recommending you to would mind you calling to arrange a meeting or having a 20-minute phone call so that you can ask them questions about their field. Make it clear that you are not looking for a job at this stage, just information.

Your career database

Keep a record of everyone you come across and their contact details – you never know when you might need to get back in touch, so it is useful to keep their information in one place. We would suggest either a spreadsheet or database (see Figure 3.1). This will give you a running overview of progress you're making, ensure you follow up on potential new leads, and you won't have to rely on your memory as to where you put their business card or when they asked you to call back if they were unable to speak when you first called.

First name	Last name	Introducer	Email address	Contact numbers	Company	Last contact	Status	Other Information
John	Gordon	Kay Williams	johngordon@ hotmail.com			Dec 2016	Call again in January	Mentioned he would introduce me to colleague James Wills

Figure 3.1

Prepare your approach

Before you start making calls to the people you have been introduced to, it is worth making a list of the information you want to gain from the conversation. Questions you might want to consider asking include:

1   How did you get into working in this field? What was your background?
2   What do you like most/least about what you do and this industry?
3   When you are recruiting someone, what skills and qualifications do you look for?
4   If you were in my position, looking to get into this career, what would you do next?
5   When you are recruiting, how do you go about it? Do you recruit through an agency, advertise on your website or in a particular publication? (This will give you a new lead on how best to apply for roles if you decide you want to go forward.)
6   Is there anything else you think it would be useful for me to know that I haven't asked? (This is a very generic question but can often yield some fascinating information!)
7   Is there anyone else you could introduce me to who could help in my search for information before I decide to pursue a career in the field?

Clearly you will want to add in your own questions, particularly targeting information that you need in order to answer any remaining questions you have from your matrix. You may also want to ask if they would mind you contacting them again if you have further questions.

Making contact

Once you have your list of questions prepared, now is the time to pick up the phone or draft your email asking for help, whichever way your contact has suggested you get in touch. When you get in contact, mention your mutual acquaintance and the fact they have helped with the introduction. Ask if it would be possible to take twenty minutes of their time either in person or over the phone to ask them a few questions about their field – again, reiterate that you are not looking for a job at this stage, it is just information gathering.

Most people are curious why you would mention that you're not looking for a job when it is highly likely you will be. The reason for this is that while most people are very happy to be helpful with information, they are usually more reticent about being put in a position where they may have to disappoint you by saying no, there is no job – they will therefore avoid a situation where that might arise. If you take that possibility out of the equation as you start your conversation, they will often relax and be even happier to help out. Don't presume that because you have got straight through to them, they are available instantly to start answering your questions – they may prefer to schedule a time that is more convenient, so it is worth asking what would work best for them.

Once you have started your information gathering interview with them and have had the OK that the time is convenient, it is up to you to manage the interview time – if you've asked for twenty minutes, stick to twenty minutes. If you are running out of time, mention that you recognize you asked for twenty minutes but you still have a few quick questions to ask, would that be OK? The person you are talking to will appreciate your consideration and will usually give you the extra time you need. When you are meeting face to face, if you want to take notes, it is worth asking whether the person you are talking to is comfortable with that. Again, most people appreciate the question and will have no problem with it.

Consolidate your information

Once your call or meeting is over, find yourself somewhere quiet to sit down and write down any additional information you want to capture, including the contact information for anyone else they've suggested you talk to. It's so tempting to think you will remember what has been said or that you'll do it later, but it is amazing how many useful gems of information can be lost by the following day. Keep revising the questions you ask at the meetings to take into account the new information you have gathered at each meeting. If you now have a picture of the qualifications you need for the role you have identified, you don't need to keep asking that same question, but you may want to ask which they consider the best place to train. As you gain more information, so your questions will become more focused and reference 'insider language', which will not only help to develop a greater rapport at this information-gathering stage but will also prove vital when you are interviewing for specific roles.

Once you have met or spoken to all of the people that have resulted from your immediate circle of friends with direct introductions, you will want to contact the people whose contact details you have but you have no introduction. Welcome to the world of networking! The contact is very similar to that above, but if you don't know anyone in common, then reference how you have come across their name (perhaps they spoke at a conference or wrote an article that you particularly liked) and you were wondering whether it would be possible for you to ask them for just twenty minutes of their time. You are more likely to get negative responses to these approaches than to the approaches where you have had a direct introduction, as there is no compunction to help you. Don't become down-hearted if you are told they can't help – it's just part of the process. It is always worth asking whether they can recommend anyone else who might be able to help in your information gathering – you never know, you might get a new contact. And it is far easier to call up a potential lead saying that you have been given their name by someone who is well known in an industry! Anything that helps is worth pursuing.

As you conclude this phase of your research, have you answered all the questions that were showing up as question marks on your matrix? Have you started to focus on one particular career option? If there are still some gaps missing in your knowledge, who can help you get the information you need? You may feel that what we are about to say next is common sense and just being polite, but it is amazing how many people don't think about the social niceties of gathering information, so we apologise if we offend those of you who would take this as a matter of course and to those who might not think about it, it's just a suggestion ... Say thank you to the person you have interviewed for information! It seems simple but it is often overlooked.

Next steps in networking

You may now have followed up everyone you can possibly think of, or you've stalled and want a new approach to keep your enthusiasm going. At this point, you might want to consider stepping into the lion's den and attend a networking meeting that is designed for like-minded individuals to meet. Try putting networking, your chosen industry and your location into your search engine and see what comes up.

Most professions have an affiliated association and this can be a good starting point. Initially you may go along to conferences and exhibitions to find out more about this field, get lists of attendees and see who is discussing the burning issues in the conference lectures or workshops. If you are doing further study as a mechanism to change career, you might use conferences as a way to help you work out what your project or dissertation should be on.

Many of the successful MBA students Jane works with use their project strategically as a way to get experience in a new field or industry. They choose a subject which is very topical and one that can be shared or partly shared with other companies in that field, so they have something to offer, if they don't get hired by the company where they are doing their project. The company with which they choose to do their project often introduces them to suppliers and partners that can be useful contacts at the end of the MBA when they are job hunting. The least successful students often just take a project offered by the business school in an area unrelated to their long-term career goals.

Case study: Klaudiusz Zwolinski

After graduating from a technical university in Poland, I moved first to Germany and then to Belgium to work for an international logistics integrator. I worked in the European headquarters in several functions in marketing and sales. The work as such was great, with challenging projects, and I worked in an international, experienced and supportive team. After a while, I started wondering if logistics was really the industry in which I would like to work for the next thirty years. I realized that I was more interested in the financial sector and so I decided to apply for an MBA to extend my knowledge, develop new skills and stimulate career change. The programme was a highly stimulating experience and enabled me to move in the direction I wanted. However, it was not easy. With no specific financial studies and a professional background in logistics, it was difficult to make the switch. The approaching financial crisis made the situation even more challenging. Nevertheless, I was persistent. An MBA project in a respected venture capital fund helped me to gain valuable insights and build credibility. I work now as an in-house management consultant in a multinational financial institution. The work is exciting and I feel pleased about the change I made. My advice for anyone is to constantly look for what you truly enjoy doing. Once you collect more experience, the picture becomes clearer but the shift is more difficult as well. An MBA or advice from a professional career coach is a very good way to put you back on the right track.

Attending a networking meeting may be a step too far for some people but we would encourage you to try if you can. If you can't, then so be it – there must be another way to get an introduction or the information you're looking for, it will just take a little ingenuity! It is always worth bearing in mind that you are likely to have to give more than you receive in terms of networking. Try not to set yourself unrealistic targets when you start networking.

When you are career hunting you are never off duty!

When you are working your way through this book, it is always useful to consider yourself continually on the hunt for information. You never know where the vital information or lead will come from that will prove to be the final jigsaw piece that helps you make the move into a new career or role. We know of several people who have won business, found a lead for a job or even gained funding from people they met in the queue at a coffee shop, starting a conversation on a train or through a fellow guest at a wedding. Again it's the case of telling people what you are looking for so they can help you if the opportunity arises.

Case study: Laura Bevill

I transitioned to a finance job coming out of my MBA through networking. My friend and mentor was someone I had met at church in Boston. He helped me prepare and apply to business schools. His former boss inquired if he knew someone who might be suitable for a new role as an investment consultant. The investment consultant had taken on a new client, a large US bank. Having written my dissertation with Lloyds TSB while at the University of Bath School of Management, the firm viewed my experience as invaluable and made me an offer. Since working as an investment consultant, I leveraged the experience and network helping me transition to represent asset managers selling to the consulting channel. I now call on people in pension consulting roles like the ones where I once worked. My new role offers more client interaction and market exposure. Today I represent Apollo Global Management, selling private equity, credit and hedge fund products to the investment consulting channel.

Remember, if you don't ask for help, you won't get it! Stretch yourself and use your powers of deduction to find all the information and contacts you need to decide whether you are ready to move in that direction. Mentors can be found in unusual places.

Amit Pandey found the networking contact who led to him applying for his first job in the UK on the cricket field. Following interviews and assessment centres he secured a job at HBOS plc as a senior business analyst. While he still had to go through the recruitment process, the initial contact came from networking to help him get a foot in the door. This was particularly impressive as he was a foreign student studying for his MBA in Leeds with no significant network in the UK.

Common concerns

Over the years, we have come across some concerns about doing this aspect of information gathering that reoccur fairly regularly, so we thought it would be useful to tell you what they are and our usual responses – so you know you are not alone, but sadly also not letting you off the hook!

What if that person doesn't want to see me?

It may happen, and if it does just move on! According to the book *Give and Take* by Adam Grant, there are takers, matchers and givers. You may have just contacted a taker who doesn't see anything in it for them. That's life. Steve Dalton goes further in his book *The 2 Hour Job Search: Using technology to get the right job faster*, in which he suggests monitoring response times to help identify those who are naturally inclined to help you (he describes them as 'boosters').

Why would they help me?

Change your mind-set. Contact them with the anticipation that they will help you. We find that most of the time, people do want to help if they are approached with courtesy and consideration. If they don't, it's a numbers game, just move on to the next contact. If however this keeps happening, then you should ask for feedback as to whether your approach or communication style could be improved.

Won't they think I work for the competition and therefore be reluctant to share information?

Most people are confident in their own ability and happy to share with others just starting out. However, if you are thinking, for example, of setting up a florist shop in your home town, it would probably not make sense to do informational interviews with other florists in the same location because they are likely to feel threatened and not want to share their trade secrets! Instead you could approach florists in towns, say, 100 miles away.

I am nervous and shy

Most people feel nervous when they start this part of the information gathering. It is a case of finding a way to work through it. Perhaps you've never interviewed people before and want to practise that before you start speaking to people in your chosen career. If so, have some fun interviewing friends about their jobs or even hobbies, regardless of whether they're relevant to what you want to do. It is about finding your confidence so that you can interview and get the information you need in a safe place. This will build your confidence to move to the next phase.

How do I find these people to interview?

Start with people who know you well because they know, trust and like you and therefore they are more likely to help you. Family, extended family, school friends, university friends, friends connected with your hobbies or sport, church contacts or people you meet at networking events – they all count. Tell them you are looking for contacts in these fields and ask if they know anyone who might be open to talking to you.

No one close to me knows anyone in this field?

Then you need to start contacting people direct. Refer back to the publications and conferences you've already sourced for names of people to contact. Now is your opportunity to start networking.

What happens if they say that they think they might have a job for me when I've already said this isn't about a job search?

Smile and say you'd be delighted to know more about the potential role. It depends on where you are in your information gathering as to whether you know if you are definitely interested in this career. You can explain why you said initially that you weren't looking for a role, just information. However, don't leap at the first job you hear about or are offered – the whole point of this book is to find the right fit for you, not just any job in your chosen field, so it is fine to express interest in knowing more but continue with your due diligence as you proceed.

I still don't know where I'm heading – what should I do?

We would love to tell you that you will get to your definitive answer on the right career for you immediately, but it often doesn't always work out that way. What we do know is that we have not met anyone who has kept the momentum and the resolve who has not ultimately come up with the answer that fits for them. If you are struggling, then this is what we would advise you to do:

I have no idea about what I have to offer – go back to the exercises in Part II and focus on your achievements to date, the transferable skills or perhaps ask close friends or colleagues what they think to get some new ideas.

I have no idea about what I want to do – go back to the matrix in Chapter 18. Can you see any ideas materializing? Perhaps it would be worth sitting down with a friend to brainstorm ideas and don't dismiss any ideas that come to mind. Sometimes it is the most unusual idea, once researched and followed up, that proves to be the answer.

I am confused – there are too many options – use the matrix to structure your research and evaluate your options against them. As you learn more through your research, you should find you are crossing some off and some others are starting to become front-runners.

I don't have enough options – brainstorm with friends, a mentor or career coach. Look online to see if there are lists of roles/sectors – do any pique your interest that might be worth looking into?

I don't know what jobs out there would suit me – you need to do more research – unfortunately there's no getting around it! The more you know about the variety of sectors and roles within them, the more you will see some options materialize.

I don't know what industry to go into – go back to the interests exercise in Chapter 13, look at websites that feature career information and narrow down the sectors that are of interest and those that are not. So you may be interested in logistics but have no interest in manufacturing or the public sector. The most important thing is not to give up.

What next?

Once you have done as much research as you feel you need to give you a clear direction, you can then move forward to the next stage. Following the research you have done, have you decided on just one option? If not, what else do you need to know to make a decision? You may have to do more research, perhaps talk to more people or go back to the brainstorming stage if you are still not sure. Once you have narrowed down your option to one that feels right, you can then start to build a strategy for next steps.

The first thing to assess is what is standing in your way of making progress towards getting the role you want. Among the things you might need to consider are:

1   Do you have the financial resources to make a change?
2   Do you need to retrain to move in your new direction? If so, can you support yourself while you retrain?
3   Do you still have some residual questions about what it would be like to work in the field? Would they be answered by further research or interviewing? Perhaps you could volunteer with an organization in the field to get hands-on experience?

We encourage you to keep gathering information until you have enough to convince you that the change you are looking at makes sense. Change of any kind is always difficult and much has been written on the subject. There comes a time for everyone who is looking to make a change in their careers to take a leap of faith. At that point it is time for action.

If you don't take this next step and keep the momentum going, your file will be full of what could have been if you had just taken the next step rather than staying put and wondering what it would have been like to have found the right job for you.

Chapter 22

Creating an action plan

He who has a 'why' to live, can bear with almost any 'how'.
Friedrich Nietzsche

The next steps you have to take will be uniquely your own. The common ones we often hear about are:

- talking to people who would be affected by your change in direction.
- building up a financial reserve or downsizing so it is possible to make a move.
- finding out about retraining and qualifications.
- arranging to go part-time in your current role as you gain experience in your new field.
- rewriting CVs in line with your new goals (see Part IV for guidance on how to do that effectively).
- creating a timeline for a potential career – what is the starting point and what are the promotion prospects?

One of the hardest things is to keep the momentum going once you have decided you want to actively take charge of your career. You have come a long way – don't give up now! Make a list of all the actions you need to undertake now and create a timeline of when you will achieve them by.

To do	How	By when	Reward
Redo my CV	Refer to Part IV and then get friend to check for mistakes	End of the month	Watch a new release film
Contact 100 companies	Research on the internet and use LinkedIn to find the right person to contact	In the next two months	Go out for dinner

We have put in a reward as it's important to stay motivated and for some people it can help. Sometimes the actual day when you start doing what you have always dreamed of feels a long way off and you need to keep motivated as you work towards it.

If you are trying to get a sense of how long you will need to commit to this, it can help to draw up a reverse timeline. That will help you stay on track and possibly change your expectations as to how long things will actually take to achieve (e.g. if you have to retrain).

Reverse timeline

Take a blank piece of paper and turn it lengthways. Create a flow chart across the page halfway down. Write your goal in the box to the far right of the page and establish your ideal date to achieve that goal. Then work your way back from right to left in three-month increments, writing down

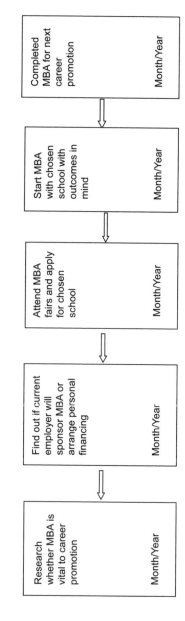

Figure 3.2 Reverse timeline example

what you will need to have achieved by that point in order to complete your goal. Keep working your way back until you have all the action points listed. Does it take you back to today? If not, does that mean you will realistically need to make more time to achieve the goal or could you shorten the time frame?

When you have decided on a goal, whether it is booking a holiday or changing your career, the next step is to plan how you will achieve it. Starting to work on your goal is a lot easier if you know what your end goal is.

Chapter 23

Returning to work

> Always bear in mind that your own resolution to succeed is
> more important than any other.
>
> *Abraham Lincoln*

Returning to the workplace – whatever the reason you have
taken some time out – can be a daunting prospect. Our
experience from working with many people in this situation
over the years is that the perception of the issues facing them
is often the biggest hurdle they have to overcome. When we
sit down and talk through all the problems they see facing
them as they try to find a new job, the list can seem endless
or insurmountable. We promise that they are not – we just
need to work out what is perception and what is reality and
then start working out how to defeat each and every one of
them. You will face difficulties. There's no getting around
that and there's no point pretending otherwise, but knowing
this you can be prepared. We have seen so many people deal
with what looked like insurmountable odds to finding a great
role for them that we have faith you can do the same. Fear
and lack of confidence can be the biggest hurdles facing those
returning to work after a break. Whether you have taken time
out of your career to parent your children, continue your
education, take a sabbatical to travel, or perhaps you were
made redundant and haven't found another job yet – the
sense of being removed from the working world and that it
has moved on without you while also leaving a gap on your
CV can keep many people from moving forward with their
search.

The exercises that we have run through so far apply to you regardless of your age, education or personal circumstances. You may have additional needs in terms of what you are looking for in your matrix – perhaps you need disabled access to the building where you work, perhaps you need to take school holidays off work, perhaps you need flexibility in terms of your hours. Whatever those needs are, it may take you longer to find the employer for you, but if you are a compelling, good candidate who is a hard worker and passionate about what you are doing, we believe you will be able to find someone who will recognize your talents and will work with you to accommodate your needs. We strongly suggest that this is your starting point.

Perceived obstacles

One of the biggest pitfalls we find when we are working with people who have been out of work for a while (when we talk about work, we are talking about the workplace rather than insinuating that anything you have been doing in the meantime hasn't been work!) is that they get in their own way when it comes to finding a job. Rather than sitting down and working out the skills they have added to their list, they focus on the skills that are outdated. At interviews, they will often spend time pointing out that they haven't worked for a while rather than highlighting what they can do for the employer and how their skill set matches those listed in the job specification.

It is important that you focus on the positive, while acknowledging any potential concerns from a future employer. If they ask about why you haven't worked for five years, don't become defensive; give a succinct, clear answer that explains why you have been out of the workplace and why you are now so keen on returning in general and to this job in particular. If for example you are asked about how you will deal with childcare (this question should not be asked, but in reality we often find it is!), again be succinct and to the point to give reassurance to the interviewer that you are in control and will not be a concern for them. Most interviewers are just trying to find the best person for the job and they are looking for you to tell them why that person is you.

Support networks

If you know several people who are in a similar position, why not set up a support network? We recently worked with a group of stay-at-home mothers who were all considering how they could start earning some money now that their children had started school. They all had different needs in terms of how much money they wanted to earn and how much time they could work depending on their childcare arrangements, but their fears were pretty similar: 'I haven't worked for ages, I've forgotten what I can do', 'There are younger versions of me who can do what I do, why would someone hire me?' 'Technology has moved on in the five years since I last set foot in an office' – you could probably continue with the list yourself. This particular group asked us to come and talk them through the exercises which they all completed and then we facilitated an initial get-together one morning to give them each a starting point with an action plan for research and exploration, building upon their matrix. They then continued to meet fortnightly, chatting between meetings if they needed help, to keep their momentum going. Three months after starting their group, two had decided to start a business from home, one trained as a virtual assistant working from home and one is hoping to retrain as a teacher. Can you find a group like this in your area? Could you start one with some like-minded people?

Chapter 24

Retirees and third age workers

Do not regret growing older. It is a privilege denied to many.

Anon.

As we are an ageing population, more people are considering working past the official retirement age. This book works whatever your age and circumstance and we encourage you, if you are in your 'third age', to look at all opportunities and consider potential new horizons rather than sticking with what you've always done.

Ageism

There's no getting away from it – ageism exists and unfortunately there will be some companies or clients who discriminate against you in terms of age at either end of the spectrum, but there are plenty who won't and often see experience as an advantage. Often it's a case of a numbers game to find the ones who are more open-minded. We have many examples of people who have found work later in life, but we have also seen people who unconsciously deter would-be employees.

If you feel being older is an issue, consider the following:

• How can you keep young-spirited? While we are not

suggesting you suddenly don the latest fashion, outdated clothes can age you. Ask someone you admire for the way they dress for some help or engage the services of an image consultant.

- What are your energy levels like? Do you look enthusiastic and motivated? Be honest with yourself. Doing work you enjoy goes a long way to helping with this and hence it's important to follow the exercises in the book.

- How can you put a positive spin on your extensive experience? What mistakes have you seen that you could help other people avoid or solutions you could suggest from your experience?

- Keep up to date with technology. Whether you like it or not, technology is here to stay and in many work environments today, it's important you embrace it if you want to stay employable. There are many different ways of learning about technology, either at local colleges of education, online or via individual tutors if you prefer.

- Double-check your own attitude to ageism. Are you expecting to come across it when you approach someone for a job? Are you presuming that you will be counted out at interview stage if you are a little older? If so, deal with those limiting beliefs before you start looking for a new job.

- Lack of experience is often an issue. Work experience can be crucial in this respect and this includes volunteering, which is often the only way to gain experience in certain fields. You may have to have a job that 'pays the bills' and fit in some volunteering to get experience in the field you want to move into.

The process is the same whether you are sixteen or sixty and we know it has worked with clients at both ends of the age spectrum.

Case study: Adrian Arnold

My father had been a very successful chartered accountant and I decided by the age of fifteen to pursue a career in a completely different field to avoid any unfavourable comparison. I had always been fascinated by medicine but I wanted to be a bit different and chose veterinary surgery as a profession. Having qualified from Cambridge University I entered general practice treating both farm and domestic animals. Within a couple of years I realized that my true love was operating surgery where the patients got better because of what I did rather than in spite of what I did. I decided to set up my practice in Crawley, which was an expanding town in need of another veterinary practice. Within a few years it had become a three-person practice specializing in small animal medicine. As the practice grew it became more profitable but, after twelve years, I began to lose the personal relationship I had enjoyed with my clients. The job satisfaction began to dip so, after considerable family discussion, we decided to 'up sticks' and start a new practice in Colchester – a part of the country I had known as a teenager. I retained my partnership in the Crawley practice while the Colchester practice got off the ground.

Computers were just beginning to become available to small businesses at the time and I got my first Apple machine to cope with the financial side of the business so I could spend more of my time practising veterinary surgery. In 1980 computing software tailored to use in medical and veterinary practices became more widely available. I saw this as a further opportunity to reduce the logistical burden of writing case histories, itemizing bills, offering quotations for future work and creating mailing lists for newsletters and vaccination reminders. This all made the practice more efficient and more profitable and gave me time to develop my interest in home computing. Unfortunately, in the mid-80s, I developed depression which became increasingly difficult to manage. I was also beginning to feel that there had been too much of a swing away from the 'art' of veterinary medicine towards the impersonal 'science'. I began to lose job satisfaction and decided to take early retirement at the age of fifty-seven.

Where to go from here? One of the pleasures of my veterinary life had been the interaction with people on a one-to-one basis. I was not really interested in how computers worked but what they could do. There was a whole generation of parents out there whose children's computing skills were beginning to leave them feeling isolated. I was self-taught in the use of computers and I had made all the mistakes of a beginner – and even some that experts had never thought of! Small advertisements in local publications soon had enthusiastic parents knocking on my door and happy to pay a commercial rate for tuition. I began to create notes on the various computing subjects that I could print out on the pupil's machine, leaving them with a hard copy that they could refer to when trying out their new skills. I was aware of the many computing handbooks on the market but the majority were written in 'computerspeak' with an unhelpful seasoning of acronyms. There was a market for a textbook written in light, humorous English which did not address the reader as either an IT student or a dimwit. My book proposal was taken up by John Wiley & Sons and the book was published in October 2008. So far it has sold more than 7,500 copies worldwide with a request to translate it into Lithuanian! Since that time I have written two follow-up books. I am now seventy-seven years old and actively following up an idea for a series of children's book based on stories I have invented for my grandchildren. If I was to offer one piece of advice, it would be that problems are only opportunities in disguise – sheep in wolf's clothing.

Chapter 25

Portfolio careers

Variety's the very spice of life, That gives it all its flavour.
William Cowper

Over the past fifteen years, we have seen a continued growth in the field of portfolio working that often offers those we are working with an opportunity to find the exact match for them. Both of us have had portfolio careers and haven't looked back since we started this different type of working – although having said that, our portfolio careers are still very different from each other's.

A portfolio career is one that is made up of a series of jobs or pieces of work that run concurrently rather than just focusing on one career that moves you progressively up the ranks of your chosen profession. A portfolio worker is often self-employed, offering a range of skills, or takes part-time employment with a few different employers. For many people, having a portfolio career is the way to integrate their various interests into their working life or a practical solution to enable them to follow their dream. Having a portfolio career might mean that for three days a week you do a job to pay the bills and then the other two days you are able to do work that pays less but gives you greater satisfaction or helps move you towards your long-term goal. It can be a great way to work in several different chosen fields and maintain a sense of independence and variety in your work life.

There are so many reasons why people choose to consider a portfolio career: they may be seeking a better work/life balance; they may want a greater variety in what they do, to explore different aspects of their skill set; they may want to avoid working for someone else again full-time – the list is endless. Tina, a journalist, was fifty-four with thirty-five years' experience in national newspapers when she took voluntary redundancy while she still had the enthusiasm and energy to start a new career.

Case study: Tina Moran

Looking back over the sixteen months since I walked away from my successful career in journalism, I can honestly say that nothing has worked out as planned. This, I now realize, is a good thing, but there were many times I didn't see it that way. At first everything seemed so simple: I would bank the generous redundancy package available after eighteen years' loyal service, take a few well-deserved months off, then accept another job, possibly on another publication or maybe as a lecturer in journalism. What I hadn't reckoned on was the massive crisis of confidence that kicked in after about three months and the fact that no matter how many jolly lunches I had with former colleagues, they couldn't simply magic up a job for me. My situation wasn't helped by the fact my marriage fell apart a month before I left my job and shortly after our youngest child left for uni. So January 1st last year found me jobless, husbandless and childless, rattling round alone in a house that had been bursting with conversation and energy just months before. I now realize my main mistake was to try to structure my future, to set out a rigid time plan of action. This was in some ways understandable; I'd been in full-time staff employment since nineteen, so a strict work/homelife routine was all I'd ever known. My initial, naive master plan went like this: Jan/ Feb, sort out my personal life; March/April, apply for jobs; May, take a nice holiday before gliding into a new job/career, possibly part-time to give me flexibility to see family and friends.

Inevitably, when this daft schedule began to fall apart early on (I was never going to sort out my personal life in two months) I started to panic. So, instead of pinging off emails for jobs I became paralysed with doubt, insecurity and fear. I wasn't sending inquiries, even to good contacts, because I couldn't face rejection and could see no reason why anyone would want to employ me. That's when I realized I couldn't do this alone and needed to build a support team – fast. For me this meant spending money on professional help – careers coach, relationship counsellor – and reconnecting with the friends I'd barely seen while working insane hours on national newspapers.

My careers coach convinced me I had many transferable skills that I simply hadn't recognized, my relationship counsellor taught me to breathe deeply and live in the moment (the sort of new age mumbo jumbo that, as a cynical journalist, I used to scoff at) and my friends helped me to have fun. I did some diligent financial housekeeping and was relieved to discover I didn't need to earn anything like I was before. I spent my retraining fund (available as part of the redundancy package) on sensible courses (web building, PowerPoint, Photoshop) and started accepting any potentially interesting work that came my way. I secured one day a week at a university media department doing basically an admin job but this progressed to a part-time lecturing position the following term. Sometimes I felt like the intern but it was challenging and rewarding to start at the bottom again. And stepping far outside my comfort zone certainly kept me on my toes. I decided to let out my children's rooms on Airbnb during term time, which has been great fun and now the house is rarely empty. And on weekends and evenings I work as a kitchen porter at a nearby cookery school – great for teamwork and delicious free food! Offers of teaching roles are now coming in from various colleges and training centres, Airbnb hosting is a lucrative and sociable diversion, I'm writing again and have been offered a lecturing role at the cookery school. So, unexpectedly, I find myself with a portfolio career, which is very exciting and has helped restore my confidence. I've learned that if you hold your nerve, ride out the inevitable confidence crash, then gradually start to rebuild on your terms, you can shape an interesting, structure-free future and I can honestly say I've never been happier.

Would a portfolio career suit you?

The idea of a portfolio career can be very compelling but there are various things that you should bear in mind if you are thinking about this as an option:

- It can be important that you maintain a strategic direction for your career – look at your portfolio as a unified whole with a direction and progression rather than as a collection of jobs that pay the mortgage.
- What activities are going to make up your portfolio? Are they viable as money-making options or will some part of your portfolio be about pursuing an area of interest?
- Do you have the time to devote to each area of your portfolio?
- Work out your household expenditure. It's really important not to underestimate the amount of money you need as this will impact heavily on the portfolio mix you are aiming for so you can see if this is realistic or not.

- What training will you need? It will be your responsibility to make sure your skills are up to date.
- Are you happy working alone? Often having a portfolio career will mean working on your own for long periods of time and many people find that this doesn't suit their personality type at all.
- How will you go about finding work? Some employers are not comfortable about employing part-time workers – can you make a compelling case for going part-time? If you are going to be a freelance consultant or have your own business, do you have the skills to go out and sell yourself? If in doubt, work out how you would sell £100-worth of your product or time – if you struggle with knowing how you would raise that amount of money, how are you going to create a solid income stream?
- Are you comfortable with uncertainty? One of the benefits of a full-time role is that you often have the feeling of security in the role (although many of you reading this may have discovered the hard way that there is very little security in full-time work if you have ever been made redundant). Constantly finding time to market yourself and deliver the work you do can be difficult and finding a balance between the two is vital.
- What additional 'protection' will you need? Most companies provide benefits for employees and if you become a portfolio worker, you will now need to consider whether you will provide these for yourself – for example, critical illness cover perhaps, mortgage protection or private health insurance.
- Are you organized? If this comes naturally to you, you are very lucky. If this is more of a challenge – think about the demands of paying bills, invoicing clients, keeping your insurances up to date, delivering on time to clients, etc. – then organizational skills are something you may want to get under control early on.

- Do you have a good support network? As you get started, you may feel nervous and, at times, isolated. Having supportive family and friends around you to help you maintain your momentum can be the difference between success and a return to your old job.
- Are you ready to become a networking expert? Once again, your ability to research and meet like-minded individuals who are also pursuing a portfolio career for advice and guidance will come to the fore. Refer back to the networking section on developing business leads within your community and through the networks you already have.

If you are determined, you will find a way to make a portfolio career work. For some that might mean taking on one part-time job that pays your living expenses and then you have one day a week to accept work from referral networks you have set up (friends and family who might refer people to you).

The hardest part is getting started and established. If you are good at what you do and professional in how you approach it, you will start to build up a good reputation and gather referrals. However we have found most people pursuing this route have to learn to market themselves. If you decide this is the option for you, keep working until you can find a balance of activities that works for you. You may make a few turns along the way that don't work, but if you have a good balance in your portfolio, you can readjust to find a turn that does.

Jane set up an eco-friendly products business ten years ago but still needed to work in her career coaching business to bring in the money to pay the mortgage. She found the mail order business took over most of her time and standing on a stall at the weekends selling her products through fairs and shows encroached too much into her family time. In the end, after much consideration, she closed the company down, as it was not making enough money to justify the huge amount of time she was putting into it. She now combines her interest in the environment with careers, with one of her webinars focusing how to develop a career in sustainability.

Over the years, we have come across so many permutations of the portfolio career that have worked well for those who have undertaken them – perhaps a few of their stories will provide some inspiration:

- Jim works four days a week as a dentist in a private practice, which enables him to take a day off in the working week and go hiking, biking or climbing in the Highlands.
- Jane took a three-day-a-week contract with a trade union to set up a career coaching service for their members, leaving the other two days free to set up her own company and find other clients
- A couple work on short-term contracts (their most recent was working at a Christmas attraction) and then at a ski resort in Canada for the rest of the time.
- Tony works as a management consultant for nine months each year and then takes three months off to pursue a new interest. Those interests have included writing a book, cycling through Europe and learning to ski.

- Chris works as an executive coach and also has a livery stables that he runs with his partner.
- Jane works as a part-time book-keeper and is retraining as a physiotherapist.
- Cora is an actor and also has a business training executives on presentation skills and communication.
- Tim writes books on personal development, advises large corporates on their HR policy (he has a background in strategic HR in financial services) and is on the speaking circuit.

Case study: Kate Clifford

Since school I have always been interested in travelling and non-profit sector work, and for that reason I did volunteer work in South Africa before and after university. At school I was also keen to specialize in something I considered a practical career, so chose to study engineering. After graduating and two years of volunteer work, even though I was still interested in social issues and working internationally, I was advised that getting some solid professional experience in engineering was worthwhile and would give me flexibility in future. I really enjoy working and living in London as a structural engineer in my twenties, and certainly learned a lot that was practical and transferable, but I was never fully satisfied. Completing a part-time Masters degree helped me to get a broader professional qualification in urban development, focusing on developing countries, and I was determined to shift my career in that direction.

My first choice was to shift incrementally, so while remaining UK-based I aimed for urban development consultancy work, gradually building up my CV while I looked for international opportunities. I started on this path and my first opening was with my existing employer looking at business opportunities for the company in developing countries plus getting some experience with colleagues in urban design and also planning and partnering with local authorities. However, within just a few months I realized I wasn't progressing or getting into the substance of the work that would really interest me. At this point I really wanted to branch out more professionally and test myself in different kinds of roles and environments, but didn't see an obvious path or employer. With Camilla's help, I took note of another long-term goal – to work for myself, for the freedom it could offer. So the big step for me was taking the plunge to go freelance. I had a plan, but not a very detailed or extensive one. I think the key in the move was to open myself up to opportunities.

The most important advice I received was to have a plan, to give myself some structure, but to take any opportunity on its merits and be ready to throw the plan out the window! I did, and, having barely written even an essay in my very maths/engineering/design-focused education, found myself utterly unexpectedly writing a guide for local government and managing case-study research on cities around the world. It was hugely refreshing, and recognizing and embracing it as a massive change meant that I resisted measuring too much if it was the 'right' step on a career ladder or whether I had the necessary credentials. It also opened up a world of new contacts that led to several contracts in humanitarian work with the UN in Afghanistan, Sudan and Indonesia – some incredible experiences.

The lesson I feel served me best since going freelance was realizing that what counted as much or more than my technical expertise was my character and relationships, my attitude to approaching new tasks and roles, and believing that there was little to lose in trying! That lesson spreads far beyond my career change; I met my partner in Afghanistan, and we currently live in Costa Rica, managing our own businesses. Based on my experiences I am also starting to coach those working in international development and the non-profit sector. The career change experience and understanding how and why I made my decisions was the foundation for the diverse life I have created for myself now that suits me really well.

Chapter 26
Starting your own business

> You will never do anything in this world without courage. It is the greatest quality of the mind next to honour.
>
> *Aristotle*

Perhaps having a portfolio career feels too indiscriminate and lacking a clear direction but you are drawn by some of the ideas discussed above. Perhaps, then, having your own business with a clear focus to make an income would work better for you. It is crucial that you do your research when setting up a business and work out your master plan. It's important to define what success means to you and where you are heading, as this will also help you decide what kind of business and what structure it should have. The things that can be so important in determining your happiness in a career can also affect you setting up a business. This can be a lonely and risky affair. The rewards can be great but you need to understand whether it will suit you. Reviewing your career can also mean that you are clear on what your priorities are – and these can change, affecting when, and if, you seek funding.

Jane's highest priority is having control of her time and this has meant she has never actively sought funding, because she always felt it would have put her under too much pressure from investors to deliver financial results. The downside of this is that perhaps the business hasn't been able to grow as much as it could have, but this was right for her at that time in her life when she had a young child. However now her son is older she is reconsidering with her co-founder how to grow the company as they want to reach more people.

Completing Part II and undertaking the research that comes from it may encourage you to consider whether to set up a business, either now or in the future. Perhaps you've had enough of working for someone else, or you have a compelling business idea that you think has legs and which you want to pursue. As part of your consideration of what's next, if owning your business is a possibility then it is well worth exploring whether, as with any possible new avenue, it will work for you.

Exploring options

By completing the process outlined in Part II you will understand what is important to you and what you have to offer. This will help you in working out what team to surround yourself with, as you will be able to see the gaps in your skill set. Additional research will help you understand the pros and cons, to see what you need to do to decide whether starting your own business is the right move for you. Some people decide that it is right in the long term for them to set up a business, so this has affected the decisions they have taken in the short term. Having said that, setting up a business doesn't have to be an 'all or nothing' approach and it is worth considering the following:

- Could you approach your current employer about setting up a new area of business? This might give you the security of a regular pay cheque while taking you in a new direction. They may even end up being your biggest client initially.
- Can you gain training or experience in a new area in your current work by putting yourself forward for new projects or pitching new opportunities for the business?
- You might be able to set up your business part-time or take

a contract initially to see if your idea has legs and enable you to keep money coming in to pay the bills.

• Your partner may be able to support you while you set up the business – a 'piggy back' approach.

Sometimes the only option is to jump in with both feet and start a business. We have found that this always seems to take longer than you think, especially if you are used to a regular pay cheque; it can be an unwelcome surprise to discover that not everyone pays on time! So make sure you have some financial reserves to get you through the early stages of setting up a business, and a good relationship with the bank for those inevitable lean periods.

Case study: Patrick Dudley Williams

'Go to room 10a' was the note on my computer screen. Ten minutes later, the only job I had ever had since university was finished. Thirteen years of 5.30 a.m. alarm clocks over, computer off, escorted out. Two days after that bombshell my wife had twins. We had a toddler, two newborn babies, a brand spanking new big mortgage and an almighty problem. It was November 2012. 'Don't worry,' I said, 'I'm going to start a company making ties.' My wife must have thought she could add 'husband's breakdown' to the list of our issues. Despite having no experience in the field, I decided to walk away from the corporate life and build a company as well as my dream job. The idea was to make silk ties that reminded people of life outside of their suit, rather than being a symbol of the corporate grind. The bonus was that I might manage to escape it myself. I'm not sure why any of my family agreed to this ridiculous idea, but I can only imagine they could see that I needed something. I knew absolutely nothing about silk ties. I just knew that they were perhaps the most boring of all clothing products, and that meant it was about time someone made them interesting again. I often heard that Sir Richard Branson saw the tie as a symbol of corporate drudgery and conformity. I saw it as an opportunity to show people there is a person behind the suit. So I went along the process of starting this little company called ReefKnots. I had virtually no money so I just figured everything out from a combination of YouTube videos, common sense and great advice. I designed everything from our prints to our packaging and even took the product shots on our website. I outsourced really specialist jobs, but most things I did myself from a little desk at the end of our bed. Often with two screaming newborns on my lap. Odd days.

In August 2013, we turned on our website and just let it roll.

Since ReefKnots has opened its doors, we've done the following (among many other things):

1   Most importantly, we've sold many thousands of ties to those wonderful customers that took a chance on us! I am in debt to every single one of them.
2   We've opened our first shop 'Knots & Socks' in the City of London at the historic Leadenhall Market. We successfully crowdfunded the project by selling store credit and products in advance.
3   I've managed to get our core product handmade in England (unlike the vast majority of our competitors).
4   We've had our ties worn by everyone from industry leaders to politicians and celebrities. We even managed to change Sir Richard Branson's mind and get him into a ReefKnots tie!
5   We've become an official corporate partner of the charity the Blue Marine Foundation, producing a special edition tie to

highlight the crisis in our oceans. We felt it important to give back to the place that inspired us.

6   We've been featured in national newspapers and on television. Ironically, I've even been on CNBC, despite never managing it when I worked in finance!

7   We've grown almost exclusively by word of mouth and social media (the 'nice tie!' effect).

8   We now sell into stores and websites across the country, with a growing wholesale business.

9   We've been named one of the Top 100 Start-Ups in the UK.

10 We've branched out into a range of new products, including the launch of our debut swim shorts range in early 2016.

It is three years since we launched and I am beginning to draw breath on a journey that was far more rewarding but far harder than anything I had anticipated.

- Listen to Patrick's story at http://thecareerfarm.com/mde46

Top tips

Jane set up her first business over fifteen years ago and has worked with numerous clients who have decided to follow a similar route. Listed below are some of their key learning points:

- Outsource what you're not good at, as soon as possible, leaving you to focus on what value you bring to the company.
- In a similar vein, recognize what skills you need to recruit; a common trap is to recruit people like you with similar skills.

- Decide on the long-term strategy of the business – easier said than done, especially if you have partners with different objectives or these objectives change due to personal circumstances. Review this regularly.
- Setting up a business can involve personal sacrifice as well as rewards – only you know whether it is worth it. Review the values exercise in Part II on a regular basis.
- Often you can be so busy delivering at the coalface you don't have time to look up and think about where the business is going – put time in your diary to do this.
- Consider whether your business is scalable and is this what you want? Do you want to have an exit strategy?
- What funding do you need? Who are you going to approach? What's in it for them?
- Consider your own personality and whether it is suited to the world of self-employment/business ownership – are you persistent enough, are you happy to work on your own initially, are you self-motivated?
- When setting up a business or bringing someone into the business, have a watertight legal agreement. Make sure this covers what happens should you disagree or circumstances change and working together is no longer an option.

Free advice is often available from banks and also more impartial advice from governmental enterprise organizations, as most governments are keen to encourage entrepreneurialism – especially when it creates jobs.

There is a whole raft of books written about setting up a business and we suggest that you do as much research as you can before deciding whether this is for you. Something else that can be helpful is to consider who your role models are and then read the biographies of the people who have been there and done that very thing.

Want to be an inventor? Read the biographies of famous inventors like James Dyson. Want to set up a shoe business? Read the biography of Tamara Mellon, co-founder of Jimmy Choo. You get the picture! Unless you are thinking about doing something really different, most of the time there are books out there that will give you insight into the type of business you want to set up. Hopefully these people will inspire you.

The impact of technology on entrepreneurs

Setting up a business has never been cheaper. Technology has had a big impact on many entrepreneurs, allowing them to run their businesses from anywhere. The advent of new tools such as WordPress has made it much more straight-forward to set up a website than previously. Cloud-based applications make expensive servers less necessary and free telecommunication services like Skype allow low-cost communication. In addition, access to affordable sophisticated email management and customer relationship management systems allows a level of sophistication which previously was only possible with a big budget. Technology has enabled the rise of the digital nomad. If you want and are able to have a flexible lifestyle, then the technology is now there to support you. Pioneers in this field such as Natalie Sisson and Marianne Cantwell (see References and Resources) have written books bursting with information and case studies of people who are pursuing a location-independent lifestyle and using technology to enable this. Websites have sprung up allowing freelancers access to a worldwide market for their skills. Entrepreneurs can work with virtual staff to make their business more productive and often reduce staff costs by buying in skills when the business needs it rather than having them on the payroll. Social media tools have revolutionized how entrepreneurs can reach potential customers on completely different continents.

AAKS produces handcrafted raffia bags in Ghana and the founder, Akosua Afriyie-Kumi has used social media to grow her brand and connect with retail stores that now stock the bags, including Anthropologie and Urban Outfitters. Read Akosua's whole story at http://www.thecareerfarm.com/mde42

Of course, one of the biggest challenges today is to be heard amid the noise of social media and to build your following, especially for a business-to-consumer enterprise. Again look at those who have done it and are in a similar position to you – i.e. they don't have a massive budget if you don't have one. Luckily again it has never been easier to reach out and connect with role models. The rise of the podcast has facilitated online learning on the go and in your own time. From a time-and-money point of view, accessing learning and potential mentors is simpler than it has ever been. It can also be useful to get advice in terms of where your role models learn from. Jane spent much of 2015 interviewing many mission-driven entrepreneurs and while they aren't on the same scale as household names like Sir Richard Branson, they are probably more representative of the size of business of the large majority of entrepreneurs. She asked each of them what business books they found useful and we share that list at http://thecareerfarm.com/reading. You can listen to more entrepreneurs' stories and career tips on the Career Farm podcast 'Grow your own career' on iTunes.

Funding

There are now more innovative ways than ever before to raise finance. Crowdfunding, for example, has opened up a whole new approach, with the added benefit of building a closer connection with your customers – or as Seth Godin would say, 'tribes'. When you have decided to invest in a company, it is more likely you will take a closer interest in what it is doing and certainly be open to further involvement – such as buying new or more products, for example.

It is crucial to choose the right sort of platform, so you will need to pay attention to how you are going to structure your offering, the type of campaign a platform specializes in, what restrictions it has and what sort of users it attracts. There are different types of crowdfunding platforms and for a business the options are principally giving away equity (so sharing your ownership) and/or giving away rewards, both in return for money. Both have pros and cons so it's important to carefully consider what will be right for you and your business. Again building your following is crucial as there are only so many times you can ask friends and family to support you!

Case study: Guy Jeremiah

I set up www.ohyo.me to make reusable collapsible plastic bottles to address the environmental problems associated with disposable bottles. Having successfully sold my first business (an environmental consultancy) I then set up Ohyo. I regularly describe entrepreneurship as a game of snakes and ladders, with one memorable snake being when I got famously savaged on *Dragon's Den*. However the next step was definitely a ladder where we went on to sell over 700,000 bottles to leading retailers in the UK. I have used two less common routes to finance the business. Instead of going the traditional route of raising finance from the banks or attracting typical equity investment, I put a team together of a corporate lawyer, graphic designer, copywriter, programmer etc.. and then gave them equity in return for their skills, retaining 60 per cent myself. Then when I developed a new product; a foldable bag in conjunction with Felix Conran, I used crowdsourcing to gain the commitment of 200 people to buy the bag before we even started to manufacture it. Both routes have allowed me to have more flexibility and control over the business direction. Listen to Guy's full story at http://thecareerfarm.com/mde15 and his crowdfunding journey at http://www.thecareerfarm.com/pod58

If you are considering the possibility of being self-employed or a business owner, it is important to point out that it is not the easy option. At the end of the day there are no guarantees that your business idea will work out, but if you do some focused thinking and research then you will be ahead of the majority of people who set up businesses, putting you in a better position to succeed.

Chapter 27

How to choose a career coach

If the impulse to daring and bravery is too fierce and violent, stay it with guidance and instruction.

Xun Zi

Career coaching

Despite the very best of intentions as you work your way through this book, you may find the going tough, lose momentum or find that your support team has fallen by the wayside. We know that while it is possible to work your way through the book to get to the answers you are looking for, sometimes it can be useful to have an experienced helping hand to give you guidance, advice and renew your enthusiasm. At that point, you may consider going to a career coach. There will be thousands and thousands of coaches in your geographic area and many will say that they do career coaching. This section will hopefully go some way to helping you sort the wheat from the chaff, decide what sort of person you want to work with and get the coaching relationship working well for you.

Coaching is definitely an investment. A good coach is all about you and your specific needs and while they may have a process that they follow, if you and a friend were being coached by someone good, you would have very different experiences, as coaching addresses what you need rather than a generic set of rules that are followed regardless. For the coaching to be at its most effective, there are two components that are vital: the ability of the coach and the 100 per cent commitment of the person being coached. If you are not fully committed, take some time to work out why and what you can do to get past it. Don't start coaching until you are absolutely ready.

How to choose the right career coach for you

Once you have decided that you would like to explore career coaching as an option, it is worth asking around your network if anyone has worked successfully with someone or knows someone who has. If not, you can contact one of the coaching organizations or contact us at www.howtotakechargeofyourcareer.com to work with us or to get the names of some suitable coaches who specialize in careers coaching rather than generalist coaches.

Before you start, it is worth asking yourself a few questions to help you narrow down the sort of person you are looking for:

- Why are you interested in career coaching right now? E.g. are you lacking motivation, are you struggling to work out the next step, are some of your limiting beliefs getting in the way?
- What is important to you in finding a career coach? E.g. experience, qualifications, recommendation, personality fit?
- What would convince you to work with someone?
- What would convince you not to work with someone?

- What sort of personality do you work well with? E.g. challenging, supportive, soft, punchy, direct, caring, safe or a combination?
- How might you sabotage the coaching relationship and are you willing to give the coach permission to call you on it? E.g. not completing your homework on time, prevaricating, etc.
- How much are you willing to invest in the coaching process financially (i.e. how much can you pay per session)?
- Are you doing this for you or is someone bribing, cajoling, strongly encouraging you to do it and you feel some reticence? If the latter, you are unlikely to get what you want out of the coaching process.

We would always advise that you talk to at least two coaches, even if someone has come highly recommended, so that you can get a feel for the different approaches coaches use and who would be best to work with you. We can't think of any coach who would not agree to this free initial conversation to discuss why you are looking for coaching and a little about you and to go into some detail about how they work.

If you go to a coaching company, make sure that when it comes to having an introductory conversation, you are having it with the person who will be your coach, not a salesperson for the company. If they are reticent to let you do that, move on!

Once you have come across a couple of names to contact, arrange an introductory conversation. It is useful if you can tell them up front what you would like to focus on and a little about you – areas might include:

- An overview of your story so the coach can get a sense of you and how you describe yourself and your background.
- Areas you would like to particularly focus on with coaching

- where are you getting stuck? What behaviours or beliefs are getting in your way?
- How would you know that the coaching has been successful?
- How much do you know about coaching – have you been coached before and if so, what worked well for you and what didn't work so well?

During the conversation there are quite a few things to think about that might help you make up your mind about who you want to work with:

- Having decided what is important to you about the coach you are going to work with, make sure you cover all those areas during the meeting.
- Coaches will have different styles/approaches to coaching, so these introductory meetings are a chance for you to see which will work best for you.
- Ask as many questions as you can – this is your opportunity to find out how the coaches work and whether you think that will work for you.
- We strongly suggest you choose the coach who you feel is the best equipped to address your reason for coaching. This may not necessarily be the person you liked the most or felt most comfortable with, although that shouldn't be entirely dismissed!
- If the coaches you meet don't seem to fit what you're looking for, it is worth checking that what you think you want really reflects what you are trying to achieve. You might also want to think about whether you are really ready to make a commitment to coaching at the moment. If you feel sure about all of that, time to talk to another coach.
- Talk about any concerns you have about the coaching with each coach you meet to see how they address them. The more honest you are from the very start, the more effective the coaching will be.

The people we recommend have a career coaching specialism and have extensive experience working in this field. Sadly we have found that accreditation and qualifications don't always guarantee excellent coaching and many coaches will agree to take on a client regardless of their level of experience in a particular specialism.

It depends what you particularly want to focus on with your coach but if it is the whole career change process, it makes sense to work with someone who has done this many times and is very confident in the field. If it is a particular limiting belief that is getting in your way, a coach with a broader skill set will be able to help. If in doubt, ask them to talk you through some examples of similar coaching assignments they have done recently.

Finally – trust your gut! If it feels right and they have the experience and you are ready to commit – go for it! If you start working with the coach and it isn't working for you for whatever reason – if you feel it is fixable, tell the coach (back to the honesty!) but if you feel it is a deeper problem, end the coaching relationship.

Cost and number of sessions

Coaching session costs vary hugely depending on many different factors including geography, experience of the coach, whether you are paying as an individual or your company is paying, and so on. Do your research at the outset to work out what the going rate is for both face-to-face coaching (more expensive) and telephone coaching (cheaper and more time-flexible) and work out what you can afford to pay. If you are going to do this, look at it as an investment; you may find the coaching gives you insights into how you can use the same methods to advance in other areas of your life and will give you a way forward for planning your career.

Coaches charge in a whole range of different ways. If you are quoted a price for a fixed programme, find out what that will cover. It is also worth asking how much any additional sessions would be if you wanted to continue the coaching and ensure you can continue with the same coach. With coaches who charge per session, it might be worth asking if they offer a discount if you buy a series of sessions together (for example, paying for the first three sessions upfront). If you go to a company that specializes in career coaching, compare their prices with those of individual coaches to make sure you are getting a good price. Some of the larger coaching companies have large staffs, premises, etc. which can boost the price per session, so it is worth checking!

We would advise that you agree to at least three sessions – in that time frame you should definitely be feeling progress and be confident that you know where you are heading. If not, tell the coach. From that point on, only you and the coach can decide how long the process will take. Some people like to do the coaching in stages (first stage to decide on new career direction and start research, second stage putting the research and networking into action, third stage making the move and so on) and others like to continue the momentum. Some people we have worked with have come up with their career change action plan within three sessions, others have taken six or twelve depending on the limiting beliefs or difficulties that can get in the way. It is not a race – it is about getting to the right place in the right time frame for you.

How to get the most out of coaching

Over the years, we have seen that the people who get the most from coaching do all or most of the following things:

- They understand that the coach is a facilitator and will not be giving them the answers but will be asking questions, giving feedback and eliciting different thoughts or thinking patterns to help create change – sadly they don't have a magic wand with the answer to your career conundrum!
- They are keen to get the most from their coaching and if they do have any concerns or things that just don't feel right, they articulate them early on in the coaching relationship.
- They give regular feedback to the coach on how they feel the coaching is progressing and how they feel it could be more effective. (If you are uncomfortable with the idea of giving feedback, discuss this with the coach as soon as possible so you can deal with this early on.)
- If they decide that it is not working for them (this may be because the coach is not right, coaching is not the right intervention or they cannot give the time required to the process), they say so and call a halt to the coaching.
- They complete all the work to be undertaken between sessions in a measured way (as opposed to the day before!) and are ready to give feedback to their coach on what has worked well and what has been less effective – i.e. they practise and research!
- They have thought through what they would like to specifically cover in that session and articulate that to their coach.
- They are open to having their thinking challenged by the coach and keeping an open mind.
- They will contact the coach in between sessions to discuss

an issue that has arisen or anything that is impeding progress so that the momentum is maintained.
- They have fun with the coaching – it can be challenging, have its difficult moments and require dedication, but it should also be fun.

Part IV: Job search strategy: Getting interviews and securing the job

> To succeed in life in today's world, you must have the will and tenacity to finish the job.
>
> *Chin-Ning Chu*

We are now on the home stretch. Our hope is that if you have followed the exercises through the book, you have:

- become aware of any limiting beliefs or people you have around you and have found a way to keep them under control as you consider what's next in terms of your career.
- an overview of your verifiable skillsets for the workplace and a clear understanding of what you are looking for in your ideal work situation.
- brainstormed various options that are worthy of exploration to check out a range of different sectors, careers, working styles.
- undertaken both active and passive research to verify whether these brainstormed options are viable for you in your current circumstances and narrowed down your future career action plan to one or possibly two specific targets.
- an action plan of how you are going to move forward with these options.

So now comes the obvious next stage: the job search strategy. Within Part IV, we will outline for you the tried and tested techniques on the basics of a job search. As with all things, you can complicate and write huge tracts on each aspect of the job search – indeed, you may well have come across huge tomes on each subject area. What we have endeavoured to do is to break down each aspect into manageable and easily achievable chunks that we have seen work time and again.

Chapter 28

What is your personal brand?

The concept of knowing your personal brand has been around for several decades but has never been more relevant than now, especially for those preparing to job hunt.

Do you know what yours is?

A quick exercise to get your thinking started:

Take a piece of paper and divide it in two down the centre (vertically). On the left hand side, write down all the things you think people say about you when you are not in the room. What would your boss say? Your colleagues? Your clients? Your best friend? The friends you see intermittently? Have a think about all aspects of how you present yourself to the world – how you are in meetings, in everyday interactions by the water cooler, how you walk into a room, the emails you send, your voicemail message on your phone ... all of the places people see you and will make judgements about what they see. Write down the good, the bad and the ugly!

Have you written down any negatives? Have you written down any positives?! You are looking to write down an objective list that is your best guess at this point.

Now on the right hand side of the page, do the same exercise, but this time write down what you want them to be saying about you in all of those settings.

How different is your list? What are the things that you would choose to change? How much do you want to change them and can you do it consistently?

Very loosely, what people say about you when you are not in the room is your personal brand and often it is not as consistent as you might think. A recent client was known in her business as a very astute lawyer and received great feedback about her ability in meetings but that people didn't really feel they knew her. One of the key things that her colleagues mentioned when a 360 assessment was undertaken (when colleagues, subordinates and managers are asked their views on your behaviour and performance at work) was that her emails left them with question marks about her. After earlier feedback to soften her email style, the lawyer had started adding a kiss (x) at the end of all her internal communications. It was so at odds with her face-to-face interactions and felt inauthentic that it had been the starting point of trust breaking down. It is a very small example of how a small thing can get in the way of how we are perceived.

We all have much more control over people's perception of us than we often choose to admit. Think about the messages you are sending out to the world and ensure you are comfortable with them. It is much more compelling to be authentic and open about who we are rather than trying to put on a persona that doesn't really serve us. This particularly gets in the way in interviews. If the interviewer meets you and you are authentic, the best version of yourself on that day, it is much easier to see if you will fit into the team or organization you are interviewing for. It may sound counter-intuitive but it is so much better to get rejected from the wrong job for being yourself than ending up in a position when you can never really be yourself. Being clear on who you are and who you want to be in the world is so much more attractive a proposition for a recruiter. So do you know what that is? Does what you wear, how you stand, how you present yourself, how you speak represent that? If you are not sure, ask those close to you for their thoughts and insights to help you develop your thinking. Are there perhaps a few small key changes you could make today that would move you closer to the list on the right side of the page from the exercise above? What would they be? Can you start today?

We have asked a best-selling author and personal branding expert to give us her views on what she sees as key when looking into this area and how to keep current. These are Jennifer Holloway's (www.jennifer-holloway.co.uk) thoughts:

When you're job hunting, your personal brand is probably the strongest card you can play to land yourself a position. You thought that would be your CV, didn't you? Well, it is in part, but your personal brand sells a whole lot more. Think of your brand as a package that offers two key things:

1) Your what (this is the functional bit)
This includes a lot of the stuff you put on your CV: what experience you have, what sectors you've worked in, what results you've delivered, what qualifications you have. It's important to have this credibility as part of your personal brand, but it's not the whole caboodle. Instead, you have to build on that with the second part ...

2) Your who (this is the emotional bit)
This is where people get to learn about who you are: the values that set your moral compass, the drivers that keep you motivated, the skills and strengths that enable you to deliver the goods, the behaviours that mark out your personality.

Time and again when I ask people, 'What was it that made you decide to give your chosen candidate the job?' their answers focus on an emotional aspect: 'I really liked their attitude', 'They said things that spoke to my personal values', 'Their personality was a great fit with my team'. These responses show it's the 'who' that seals the deal. (Of course, you have to be able to do the job in the first place, so the 'what' can't be ignored, but don't make it the entire focus when you're selling yourself.)

That ability to sell both the what *and* the who is why your personal brand is so important. For example, I had a client who lost out on a top job on two occasions, despite a strong CV and lots of practical examples to back up her interview answers. The feedback she received from the agency who'd put her forward was: 'They had complete confidence you could do the job, but no idea of who you are.' Of course, you don't have to save your personal brand for the interview room. If you're canny, you'll be giving clues to who you are well before you're in the hot seat: Here are some areas to consider:

Your CV

Think about the font you use: different typefaces convey different messages, from youth to gravitas. When you include your contact details, make sure you don't shoot yourself in the foot with a negative email address (partygirl@hotmail.com isn't a good idea). It's also recommended to include the address of your LinkedIn page (which is a must for anyone looking for a job) to provide extra detail that you wouldn't include on a CV – such as a photo and recommendations. And always, ALWAYS, ensure what you've written is 100 per cent accurate, because nothing gets a CV deposited in the bin faster than a spelling mistake.

Your online footprint

I've spoken to countless recruiters who say that once a person's CV has convinced them the candidate is worth considering, they immediately hit Google to find out more. As one said: 'If their online footprint doesn't live up to initial expectations, that's an immediate fail.' LinkedIn is the first place to get it right. Your picture should look the same as you would when you walk into an interview – so no snaps of you in a bar or at a wedding. And always include a summary, as it's exactly the place where you can include insight into who you are, alongside the factual stuff. Plus think about all the other places online where you exist and make sure you're careful and aware (not overtly criticizing anyone or using obscene language) or have your privacy settings set to full strength.

Your initial contact

It's a common mistake that people spend all their time preparing for an interview by practising their answers to the expected questions. Instead, you should allocate just as much time to thinking about the bit before the interview itself. Start by planning what you're going to wear and make sure it's not only clean and ironed, but also has a hint of your personality about it, whether that's from the pattern of your tie or the colour of your shoes. Practise your handshake, coupled with good eye contact and a beaming smile, to immediately convey warmth and confidence. Lots of people think they have good handshakes but they're often too weak or too strong, so get some feedback. And remember that every question is a chance to make an impact. If you're asked, 'How was your journey?' don't just say 'Fine thanks'. Think about how you can add some personality, such as: 'It took an hour on the train but I'm reading a great book at the moment, so the time flew by.' They'll ask you what you're reading, you start up a conversation, and all of a sudden your personal brand is working its magic. All that before you've even answered the first interview question!

Chapter 29

What you want from a career versus what an employer wants from you

> Do not hire a man who does your work for money, but him who does it for love of it.
>
> *Henry David Thoreau*

It may sound obvious, but one of the things that so many candidates fail to appreciate is that what they are looking for in a new role is often not necessarily what an employer is looking for to actually fill the role. You may well have identified that you want additional responsibility, an opportunity to advance, increased salary and benefits, better work/life balance perhaps, and so your list will continue – look at your matrix for your personal list. From an employer's point of view they may well have a distinctly different list of requirements when they are filling a role, which might include someone to solve their immediate problems in the business, a square peg to fit a square hole, someone to save and/or make them money, a fully committed worker and ultimately someone who will make the employer's job easier.

There is room to satisfy both sets of needs but it is important to bear in mind, as you start your job search, that when you meet a potential employer, you focus on their needs rather than yours and what you can bring to the job, not what you are personally going to get out of it. We will focus more on this during our overview of giving a good interview, but it is a good rule of thumb to keep in the back of your mind in all your interactions 'What can I do for you?' rather than 'What are you going to provide for me?'

Chapter 30

Applying for jobs

The job market is huge. Even in a downturn there are new opportunities constantly appearing – you just need to know where to look. Most job seekers rush around like headless chickens applying for everything and anything. A more effective approach is to use routes to market which fewer people use.

In the following chapters we have outlined a range of different strategies for your job search and will encourage you to look at a variety of approaches to achieve your goal of a new role. There are two key aspects to the job market: the traditional open market (applying for jobs through advertisements and recruiters) and the hidden market (finding jobs through networking and speculative applications). According to a study by Drake Beam Morin, a world-leading provider of strategic human resource solutions, 64 per cent of those surveyed said they found their new jobs through networking. This figure is commonly cited by recruiters and outplacement firms, which is why we have started with that as our first recommended strategy. Companies want to keep their recruitment costs down (which can be up to 33 per cent of an employee's annual salary in some cases) and they want to hire 'known' quantities – people who have been recommended to them, whom they have seen in action or who have an excellent reputation in the market. As well as a potential reduction in cost, a direct approach from a motivated candidate who has done their research or a recommended candidate reduces the risk for the employer of hiring the wrong person, resulting in a quicker hire with less time spent filtering out unsuitable candidates.

Chapter 31

Networking

> It's not what you know but who you know that makes the difference.
>
> *Anon.*

First, it is important that your networking is targeted, as networking without any kind of target will generally be a waste of your time. By this stage in your research, you will have a list of companies you want to target in your chosen sector. It depends on your specific job search as to how many should be on your list. For example, if you are looking for an IT help desk role in a large company, there are often several of these roles, so you will probably need a smaller list. If you are looking for a global HR director role in a large company, there may be just one position, so you will have to spread your net wide to uncover opportunities. For each company, find out if there is someone there you know; if not, look at your research for possible contacts you have come across.

In Jane's recruitment days, the company she worked for used a metric of 200 CVs sent out in order to get eight interviews, which resulted in two or three job offers. So you can see why we encourage you to increase your volume of applications, although we must stress: don't lose the quality – people can tell when they are just part of a mail shot, so tailor each application.

While we are advocates of using business networking sites and have seen clients gain projects, consulting work and jobs through these sites, it can be all to easy to hide behind them. There really is no substitute for meeting people face-to-face, as this really can progress your career. When you arrange a networking meeting, it is useful to approach it as a business meeting where both you and the person you have arranged to meet will benefit. They may well have important information about the industry, firm or even potential job opportunities that could be vital to your job search but that they may also benefit from themselves. The more of these meetings you have, the more information you will gather and – provided it is not confidential – you can share that in future meetings to create more of a two-way experience. This is about gathering information and asking for advice, not about asking for a job outright or begging for help!

Marketing and positioning yourself if you have a lead into the company

Once you have found the appropriate contact within your network, ask them for the background information you need on the target organization (but not information in the public domain) and the name of the person to whom you should address your application. If you are able to refer to your contact in the application letter, so much the better – it will add credibility to your approach. Business networking sites like LinkedIn (www.linkedin.com) are useful to help you ascertain whether there is anyone in your network who may be able to help you connect with a contact in your target organization.

When approaching people for a networking meeting, it's not advisable to send them a copy of your CV unless they have specifically requested it. A CV can immediately flag up to a networking contact that you are looking for a job; if he or she doesn't have any immediate jobs, they might not see you. At this stage you want to meet them to find out how your skills could meet their needs and so a better approach is to write a carefully crafted introductory letter which emphasizes your relevant experience. We suggest you consider sending a letter rather than an email (unless the recipient knows you will be emailing them). This is because people are wary of receiving emails from unknown sources and also, given the large volume of emails received by managers, your communication may not receive the attention it deserves.

As a guide, if you have relevant past work experience, we advise that your letter follows the following format:

- The first paragraph introduces you and states the name of the person in your network who has provided the introduction.
- The second paragraph comments on an area of interest that the company is currently facing, which you have identified in your research (perhaps you've noticed they have just launched a new service or expanded their operations in a new location).
- The third paragraph states how your past work experience is relevant in connection with the area of interest.
- The final paragraph details how you are going to follow up for the purpose of organizing a meeting or conversation.

If you don't have relevant past experience, you can use the above format but in the third paragraph you need to refer to either the project/internship/volunteer work you have done or you are planning to do and how it is relevant to them.

Follow-up tips

You should follow up your letter ideally about a week after it has been sent – any earlier and you might look pushy, any later and they might have forgotten about you.

Following up with a phone call will increase your chances of getting a meeting. A simple technique for overcoming voicemail is to leave just one message stating that you are following up from your letter. If they don't return your message after a few days, keep calling them until you get hold of them, but don't leave a message if you get voicemail again. If you keep leaving messages you might be perceived as a nuisance. A secretary or PA can help you get in touch with them if you are polite and ask for the best time to ring in order to get hold of the person. Another strategy is to call early in the morning or late in the evening. You may have more luck getting through to the person you want to speak to, and if you have encountered an unhelpful secretary or PA, he or she is less likely to be there.

Meeting tips

If you are successful in securing a meeting, how do you get the most out of this precious opportunity?

- Try and get to the venue early but go to a cafe until the right time, to ensure you are on time.
- At the outset reiterate who you are, why you are there and who has suggested you get in touch to create a shared point of contact. It is useful to have an outline agenda of the meeting in your head before you start so that you know what you want to cover and preferably in what order. This

will allow you to cover all the important areas during your meeting while also finishing on time.

- Your mission for the meeting is to find out if there are any potential jobs or ways into the business and how to pursue those opportunities.
- Be sure to ask as much as possible about them and the issues facing the company so you can work out how to position yourself. Do your research before the meeting to prepare some good and pertinent questions.
- Like an informational interview, if you've said that you will only take up 20–30 minutes of their time, it is up to you to keep an eye on the time of the meeting and make sure you stick to the time you have requested.
- When you are at the end of your meeting, it is always worth asking if there is anyone they could introduce you to, who may be interested in talking to someone with your background. If they do come up with new contacts, take the initiative and ask them to let their contact know you will be in touch rather than waiting for their contact to get in touch with you. If you say you are going to follow up these leads – make sure you do.

After struggling to get through to the CEO on the phone, John rang at 7.30 a.m. and succeeded. He asked if he could come in for a chat the next day and he assured the CEO he would not take more than 30 minutes of his time. During the meeting John asked lots of questions, one being what problems kept the CEO awake at night? When describing the issues the CEO gave John lots of ideas for projects. He wrote to the CEO after the meeting and put forward a proposal to investigate and present a solution to one of the major problems the company had. This was accepted and at the end of the project John was offered a permanent job.

Always follow up after the meeting with a letter or email to thank them for their time. Depending on the content of the meeting you might want to mention the issues you covered, write a short proposal on how you could work for them or, if appropriate, reiterate how your experience could assist them. Make sure you keep in touch and send them any information that might help them with their job or a current issue they are facing.

Speculative applications: Marketing and positioning yourself if you don't have a lead into the company

The advice regarding the type of letter you should write, the format, how to follow up and conduct a meeting is the same as for the section above, except you won't be able to refer to a mutual acquaintance. This means it is even more important to follow up your letters. This will give you the opportunity to find out if you have sent your letter to the right person. Make sure you personalize a direct approach letter: make reference to changes in the industry, issues the company may be facing, or even the fact they have got a new job! Think like a consultant – how can you demonstrate that your skills can help them?

If you are not able to identify a contact within your network who can help you with your target company, you will need to make a speculative approach – a direct approach to someone you don't know. Contacting people 'cold' is a method that many of our clients have used successfully but you must be realistic and make sure you keep your volume of applications high; this is very much like a sales cycle – you have to feed the pipeline to uncover opportunities. Also as we have said, depending on the role you are targeting (e.g. for a senior position there will be fewer roles) you may need to increase the number of companies you approach.

Make sure you are targeting people at the right level for the type of work you wish to do. Ideally aim two levels above the level you want to work at. If in doubt, target high but not too high, as a letter that has been passed down from someone senior is more likely to be taken seriously, but just writing to the CEO of a large plc is likely to be passed to the human resources department by his or her PA. Bear in mind you don't want your CV falling into the hands of a manager at your level of seniority who sees that your experience is better than his or hers – then it could end up in the bin!

Unless you want to work in human resources, we advise our clients to write to line managers where possible. If the company has a clear recruitment policy then naturally you will need to abide by these rules, but otherwise line managers are close to the business and are in a good position to see when job opportunities might arise in their departments. A senior marketing manager within a well-known plc told us that she keeps all good unsolicited CVs and meets some senders for a coffee, as she never knows when she might need good people in her team.

Make sure you are regularly scanning the press (including industry magazines) or are signed up for alerts for articles connected with the companies in your target list. This can give you an appropriate contact name, as senior people are often quoted in articles.

Other places to find the names of senior executives include:

• The press and magazines related to the industry in which

you are interested. These often announce new appointments. It is also worth noting that people new in position may be open to recruiting new people.

- The company's annual report.
- The company's website.
- Speaker lists from industry conferences.
- LinkedIn (www.linkedin.com). Search on company and job titles and scan testimonials given by managers of people working for the target company as they will often lead you to more names.

Chapter 32

Job fairs

Job fairs are generally targeted at the more junior end of the market, as well as targeting specific skills which companies are trying to recruit, e.g. technical skills. Fairs are a great way to get a feel for an industry and meet representatives from companies. Sometimes the representatives are from human resources and sometimes they are line managers, but either way you can have face-to-face conversations and it is an opportunity to build relationships. The downside is you are getting the sanitized version of what it is like to work for the company, not what it's really like! However by using tools like LinkedIn, you have the opportunity to reach employees who may be able to give you the inside track or, even better, past employees who are often able to be really open about the pros and cons of a company.

- Take your business card and several copies of your CV.
- Go early – representatives may be less tired than later in the day so more likely to help you, and it might be easier to be memorable.
- You need to stand out; the best way to do this is to ask insightful questions, having done your research. Don't ask questions you could have answered by an internet search. Ask their opinion, ask them why they joined the company, what work they do, what kind of assignments are on offer.
- Take your 'A' game, look smart – shoes polished, clean nails, tidy hair, as if you were going for an interview. Do your homework – software companies will have a different dress style to investment banks.

- If there is rapport, ask if there is anyone else they could recommend you speak to. Ask for their business card and follow up with them.
- When you follow up make sure you remind them who you are. Perhaps you asked unexpected but insightful questions or had clearly done effective research. That person will have met a lot of people at the fair, so you need to jog their memory.
- Don't monopolize their time. If you sense they are feeling like you should be moving on, politely say you don't want to take up too much of their time and signal you are on your last question.
- Make sure you personalize your request to link to a contact on LinkedIn. Many recruiters we know won't accept a linked request that someone has not bothered to customize. Make sure you send the request from a device that allows you to customize the request.
- Follow the contact on Twitter as well, as long as it's a business account. Many recruiters now have their own Twitter account. You should be following the company on all the social media platforms you are active on.

Job fairs are one route to market. Like advertising, there is a lot of competition and often it's only the bigger companies that have the resources to attend job fairs. So don't overlook small and medium-sized companies.

Chapter 33

Advertising

Responding to job advertisements is the most obvious way of getting a job, but it is also the most competitive. With the advent of internet advertising, employers get hundreds if not thousands of applications. If you are looking for a role that builds directly on your current experience, then responding to job advertisements should be an important part of your strategy. It is also important to consider if you are changing industry, as sometimes functional experience is more important to recruiters than industry experience. However, if you are completely changing career then, unless you're willing to start at the bottom, this method of job hunting should be your lowest priority.

Jobs advertised in newspapers

Although the main newspapers do have websites, it's best to buy the newspaper on the day its appointments section is published as there can be a delay in putting vacancies on the website. Newspaper websites have alerting facilities that allow you to register what kind of jobs you are interested in. Matches will be emailed to you as they are placed on the site.

How and why to read job adverts

There are two reasons to read the job adverts. The first is obvious: to find that dream role that matches your skills and chosen career perfectly. The second is perhaps less obvious: it can be a great way to keep in touch with the market and can form an important part of your ongoing research.

When you are reading a potential advert that seems to match what you are looking for in your next role, it is worth using a highlighter pen to make sure, when you respond, that you have covered all the key areas. They include:

1 Any reference number or name of the advertisement – make sure you include this in your application so the recruiter knows which job you are applying for.
2 Skills and experience that are essential to the role – highlight each of them so you can make sure that both your covering letter and CV feature those skills prominently.
3 Additional skills and experience that are desired but not essential – if you match them, it is worth highlighting the fact in your application.
4 The application deadline date – if not stated, the deadline is often two weeks post ad. The sooner you apply the better, as sometimes recruiters will stop reviewing applications when they receive enough.

If you are reading the adverts but not finding the role for you, look at the companies who are advertising in your chosen sector or function. Are they on your list of potential future employers? Do they always recruit directly or through a recruiter? Are you starting to see a recruiter that specializes in your industry who you have not been in touch with? What are the typical salaries being advertised in your chosen field? You never know when an advert might help you spot a new opportunity for your job search.

Chapter 34

The world of recruitment companies

Recruitment firms are most interested in people who have relevant experience for the position they are trying to fill. Therefore, these firms will be useful tools for you if you're looking for a role that builds on your previous experience. Remember that functional experience (such as finance skills, HR skills, etc.) is often transferable across industries, so don't discount recruitment firms if you're looking to stay in the same function but in a new sector.

If you don't have a lot of relevant experience, it is likely to be more profitable for you to use networking and speculative applications as your principal methods of job hunting.

It is useful to explain how the recruitment industry works so that you can decide your strategy when dealing with them. When a company decides to recruit via a recruitment firm then the firm will use one or more of the following methods:

Database search — The recruitment firm searches their database of candidate CVs to find a match for the open position (typically used for lower level positions).

Advertised selection — The recruitment firm places an advertisement in a relevant publication or on the internet (used at all levels for positions with salaries of up to about £100,000).

Search/headhunting The recruitment firm directly approaches (headhunts) individuals (typically used for senior positions, where the appointment is sensitive, or for skills that are difficult to find). The individuals approached are usually well known within their industry, or are identified by researchers working for the recruitment firm.

Companies which specialize in recruitment are generally split into two different 'camps': agencies that do something called contingent recruitment, i.e. they are paid only if one of the candidates they have introduced is hired; and search firms who are paid an ongoing retainer for the research phase as well as the introduction of the successful candidate. All recruiters, but in particular executive search consultants, receive many unsolicited letters and CVs, and relatively few people who approach them are invited for interview. So if you have an introduction to a search consultant we suggest you use it, as you are then more likely to be invited in for a chat.

Who the recruitment firm represents

A common misconception is that the recruitment firm is there to represent your best interests as a candidate. Over the years, we have heard many people bemused at the lack of attention they get from their recruiter unless they look like they are a 'sure thing' to get the job they have been put forward for. It is important to remember, however, you are not the client. You are just one of many candidates they have access to and can introduce. As it's the company recruiting that pays the bill, they are considered by the recruitment firm to be the client and that is where they focus their attention. You are, with the best will in the world, a commodity. It is your job to show them how valuable a commodity you are, to maintain contact and help them in their job to impress their paying client. The fee paid to a recruiter is usually a percentage of the successful candidate's annual salary – typically 20 per cent for database (the percentage often increases with salary), 25 per cent for advertised selection and 33 per cent for search/headhunt. Another reason why a direct approach can often be a cost-effective option for hiring great candidates! It may be a contentious thing to say – and clearly this is not true of all recruitment consultants – but because they are rewarded by the number of people they place in employment, this is where their focus is almost always centred. Many candidates have hopes that a recruiter will also offer careers guidance and, occasionally, to think outside the box in terms of the roles they are put forward for. This rarely happens and often leads candidates to feel that they have not had a great service from their recruiters. Again, remember that you are not the client – you are a very useful piece of the puzzle if you have the skills they are looking for. If you understand the key drivers of most recruiters, it is easier to limit your expectations and help them provide the right candidate to their client – you!

The best headhunters to approach

Most recruitment firms are organized into specialist functions – e.g. IT, marketing, finance – and then each consultant within the firm will specialize in certain industry sectors.

Ask people in the industry or function that you want to work in which recruitment firm they use and who they rate in the market place – again, it helps if you have a warm lead into the recruiter by mentioning that one of their clients has suggested you call. Even if you are not looking to be hired at the moment, keep a folder of advertisements for the type of roles you are interested in. Make a note of the name of the recruitment consultant if it is given, as often when a consultant moves on he/she will keep the client relationship. In the recruitment industry, consultants may move companies frequently – often moving on to recruit at a higher level – so you need to keep track of where the people who recruit in your field are working. Recruitment consultants also often work on assignments which are never advertised so it is worth trying to develop a relationship with the key players so that they think of you when a suitable role comes up either as a candidate or as a potential source of research they can ask to find the ideal candidate. Building these relationship will be useful for your whole career. There are thousands of recruitment firms so you must be selective, contacting only those that are relevant to you. If you are trying to change function as well as industry, remember you should use the networking and speculative applications to get a job, as recruiters are unlikely to be able or willing to help.

If you are an experienced executive, you might want to consider 'interim recruiters'. Organizations often need additional resource if they have a specific project to deliver or need someone to join the team who can 'hit the ground running' and have very specific experience in that field. Interim management is all about implementation rather than consultancy, which is about working with a client to give advice. It can be a great way to get experience in a new sector while using your experience in a specific function.

If you are just starting work or have limited work experience, you may also want to consider temping – fulfilling temporary assignments to cover holidays or a work overload. Most recruitment companies have interim or temp divisions so you may also want to investigate this as an option.

Sites like www.upwork.com can offer even more flexible work, but you are likely to need a specific skill set such as programming or design.

Tips for dealing with recruitment firms

Most reputable recruitment firms follow best practice; however it is wise to ask the recruitment firm to contact you before they send out your CV to a company. This is to make sure they don't send your CV to a company that you are already trying to contact through networking or direct marketing. This can sometimes happen and may result in your new employer having to haggle about whether they have to pay a fee to the recruitment firm who may claim to have introduced you. If you are looking to use your relevant experience, recruitment consultants are constantly active in the market, and know the companies who are hiring. Like any industry, there are bad consultants, but, contrary to popular belief, there are great ones too and certainly an important potential route to getting the job you want.

Marketing and positioning yourself with recruitment firms

When you have selected the recruitment firms which are most appropriate to you, send them a copy of your CV which is specifically targeted to the job you want to secure. Your covering letter should state what role you are seeking and where you wish to work. Giving this information saves time and helps the recruiter consider you in relation to what his or her clients might be looking for. Make sure you include what salary (plus other benefits such as bonuses or car allowances) you were on in your last role, as you will be asked about this, and make sure you clearly state any geographical restrictions you have, which saves time all around. Again your covering letter must clearly state what you could do for the recruiter's clients, making it easy for the recruiter to 'sell' you in.

Chapter 35

Covering letters

Grammar is the grave of letters.

Elbert Hubbard

A covering letter (i.e. a letter or email you send in response to an advertisement or potential job situation to accompany your CV) is an important aspect of your application. Unless stated, we recommend a covering letter is always sent when you apply to a job. It is your chance to establish why you are writing and to encourage the interviewer to read your CV. You have the opportunity to highlight the skills you have that match the skills the interviewer is looking for and why you would be an ideal candidate. The letter will be similar to those you might write for networking or to secure a meeting via a direct contact; however, in this case you know what the interviewer is looking for. Interviewers have a very short period of time to make a decision about whether to invite you in for a meeting, so it is imperative that you are very clear about how you meet the recruitment criteria.

We recommend covering letters should be one page, to the point, and should ideally follow the format below:

- The first paragraph explains what job you have applied for and why you have applied.
- The second paragraph briefly summarizes your background.
- The third paragraph highlights the skills you have that match what the company is looking for (ideally in an easy to read bullet point form).
- The fourth paragraph gives any extra information asked for in the advertisement.

- The final paragraph is your sign-off and says that you will either contact them or request they contact you to arrange an interview or to discuss next steps.

If you meet every single criterion stated in the advertisement, then you can use the 'mirror technique'. Do this by listing the required attributes on the left hand side of the page, and then opposite each one show a specific example of how you meet the requirement. When making the list on the left hand side, try to use the same words and phrases that are used in the advertisement. The mirror technique is beautiful in its simplicity!

For example:

I list below how I meet the criteria for the role:

Strong track record in sales – For the last two years over-achieved sales target by 150 per cent.

International experience – Remotely managed twelve sales staff in Hong Kong, while based in London. Travelled as General Manager responsible for EMEA.

If you don't meet all the criteria listed in the advertisement, just list in one column the ones you do meet. Be as specific as possible and avoid vague phrases; recruiters look for hard evidence. This approach can be used for all advertisements and positions that are advertised by recruitment firms. If you would like a free template please go to http://thecareerfarm. com/cover.

Most people think of some well-worn phrases as to why they want to work for that company – phrases they have lifted off the website ... not that impressive! If you want to stand out as a serious candidate, demonstrate your in-depth research into the company, perhaps giving some insight into their position in the market or a recent piece of positive news about them. Even better is mentioning someone you have taken the time to meet to understand the culture of the company – this really shows you have done your due diligence. Make sure that you have highlighted key parts from your experience and skills that are relevant to the role you are applying for. Avoid mentioning any aspects of the job advert that you do not match such as your age range or lack of degree, detailing skills that are not relevant to the role, or the salary you are looking for, unless specifically requested. Always, always, check spelling and grammar. Finally make sure your covering letter isn't too subservient. You should be equal partners in a decision to be hired and your covering letter is a good indication of how high your self-esteem is and whether you have a professional approach. A good covering letter says that you are organized, logical and know what value you will bring to the table. Using the 'mirror technique' demonstrates a logical mind, a mature understanding of what the recruiter is looking for, and the key thing the hirer needs to know at this stage, which is: do you have the experience for the job so that I can invite you in for interview?

Chapter 36

CVs/resumés

Your CV (also referred to as a resumé) is a vital tool in your job search armoury. It is your chance to sell yourself and your skills in a clear, simple, interesting and impactful way. A well-written CV will help you get an interview, focus the interviewer on your pertinent achievements and give them a clear overview of what you could do in this role for the hiring organization. If you are sending your CV in response to an advertisement, especially in a market where that role may get many responses, your CV and covering letter may get no more than a cursory look. An interviewer will usually separate the CVs into three different piles:

- the interview pile (CVs that look promising and highlight achievements matching the job specification).
- the hold pile (CVs that have potential if there are not enough candidates in the interview pile).
- the reject pile (CVs that do not hold the attention of the interviewer).

For competitive jobs often the hold pile won't get used. So how do you get in the interview pile? It is important that you stand out in a good way and we have set out below some key criteria that we know are effective in achieving this.

Compiling your CV

To make the recruiter's life easier, if you are sending your CV by email you should save it in a Word document, as your full name. If you are going to change it, attach different version numbers to it – e.g. Andrew_SmithCV1.doc. That way, if a company rings you once they have had your CV for a while, you can check which version they have and send them an updated copy. Again, it may seem obvious, but also don't password protect your CV! Unless you are an incredibly compelling candidate that the recruiter has heard of, you are more likely to have your CV deleted than someone coming back to you to ask you for the password.

A good rule of thumb is that if you have less than five years' experience you should be able to get your CV onto one page; if you have more experience you will probably need two pages. Even if you have many years of experience, you should be aiming for two pages with three as an absolute maximum, as your earlier career history is unlikely to be as relevant so can be summarized. The only true variation to this is for academics, whose CVs are traditionally longer with a full list of published articles etc. Recruiters are most interested in the detail of what you have been doing for the last five years, so make sure this is what you emphasize; just writing a couple of bullet points for a position you were at for the last four years is not helpful.

Different parts of the world have slightly different formats or idiosyncrasies. The most common CV we see and which is accepted by major companies worldwide is a reverse chronological CV. This means your experience is displayed with your most recent roles first.

It sounds obvious, but all your CV needs to do is make it to the interview pile. People often try and do too much with their CV, believing it will get them the job.

Here are our top CV secrets which we've gathered over the years with the assistance of leading global recruiters, HR professionals and line managers responsible for hiring:

Make sure your CV has achievements as well as responsibilities listed and that these are evidence-based.

Is there some evidence you can point to that proves you have the experience and the skills for the role you are applying for? Where possible, start your bullet points with 'action verbs', e.g. initiated, managed, presented, led.

Achievements are key in deciding between candidates and are often missed out. If you consider two managers of Manchester United Football Club, Sir Alex Ferguson and Ron Atkinson both had the same job responsibilities, but had a very different list of achievements.

Always write in the past tense not using the word 'I'.

For example:

Achieved a 30 per cent increase in sales in the first six months by developing existing accounts.

Rather than:

I was a member of a team involved in developing existing accounts.

Use a profile with caution

A profile is a paragraph, often at the top of a CV, which positions you in the eyes of the reader. It highlights key selling points or makes clear any ambiguity in your experience.

The jury is out about whether interviewers read these profiles – some like them, some are ambivalent – so unless it really adds something to your CV leave it out. Too many profiles are full of phrases such as 'brilliant communicator' or 'good team player'. These words may be true but they are only your opinion and not backed up by hard evidence, so effectively they are worthless statements! When you are making statements, especially in a profile at the beginning of your CV, make them objective rather than subjective – the reader should be able to look down your CV and find evidence to back up each of your claims.

Here is an example of a profile for a career changer (charity sector to commercial sector) which wasn't working:

> I have a strong track record of working in challenging situations; understanding and meeting the needs of diverse stakeholders and delivering results. My strengths are in analysis, persuasion and leadership. I believe my MBA has further developed my business skill set and will enable me to make a significant contribution in the demanding, fast-paced marketing position I seek. I am a dynamic communicator who is always respected by the teams I have worked with.

And one that was on a CV which secured an interview:

> MBA marketing graduate with 10 years' experience of managing 'charity brands'. Extensive experience of running international teams of over 30 permanent and volunteer staff, managing key change programmes and communicating with key stakeholders.

As you can see in the second example, the candidate positioned himself with greater clarity. He explained his background to the reader, highlighting the skills relevant to the job he was applying for, and used more evidence than the first version.

If you do use a profile, we suggest it is between three and four lines long and that it is a good overview of you and your skills. It should also highlight the particular skills you have that are identified as important to the role you have applied for. It can be a good way to ensure that the reader is in no doubt that you match all of the key requirements they are seeking.

Use bullet points to make your CV easy for the reader to scan your experience.

Long paragraphs are hard on the eye, making it difficult to pick out the relevant experience.

For everything you put on your CV ask yourself – so what?

You need to be able to justify in your own mind everything on your CV, so when you put down a bullet point, ask yourself: So what? What was achieved? What did that action lead to?

There is no rule to say you have to mention all your responsibilities and achievements, so decide which are most relevant to the job you are applying for. You may have several CVs for different job applications that cater for this.

If you include them, what do your interests say about you? Typical endurance events such as marathons show persistence and resilience. While interests are not recruitment criteria, this could make the difference if there are similar candidates and it gives some indication as to how you might fit in with the culture of the firm. Camilla was down to the final two for a role in banking and the line manager eventually offered her the role because she played the cello and so did he – he said that he couldn't split the candidates in any other way and thought they might at least have something in common!

The first two bullet points position you

Make sure you prioritize your bullet points and take particular care over which bullet points come first, as these first two really position you to the reader.

Presentation of your CV is important

When you are preparing your CV in terms of its layout, make sure:

- The font is readable (font size should be no less than a pitch of 10.5) and the layout is uncluttered with plenty of white space. This will all make your CV much easier to read.
- Use short, succinct bullet points rather than paragraphs of text.
- Spell check and then get a pedantic friend to read through your CV checking and double checking for any spelling or grammatical errors.
- If your CV runs to more than one page, put your name and contact details in a footer on all pages so that if the front page should get separated, the company can still get hold of you.
- If you are taking your CV in hard copy to an interview, use white paper and avoid using a binder or staples to keep it together.
- In some parts of Europe it is more common to use a photograph on a CV, but in the UK we would not recommend attaching a photo. Again, it is worth researching the accepted format in your location.

Always be honest

Never lie about your experience, qualifications or indeed anything on your CV – we have seen many examples where what a candidate thought was a fairly minor lie has led to a job offer being revoked. It is not worth the risk and any lie that is discovered will cast you in a negative light.

Your CV should reflect you

When you have written your CV, have a final read through

and check that you really feel that it reflects you well and you are comfortable with it. It is your marketing document and so it is important you are pleased with it. There are CV writing services available in the market but we advise our clients to stick with writing their own for a couple of reasons. First, the CV writer will never truly know you and your experience as well as you do and a small change of nuance through lack of understanding can be important. Secondly, good recruiters can often spot when the CV has been written to a format by someone else (some can even tell which firm has written the document) and are often not flattering about the results.

Use a professional email address

When you put your contact email address on your CV, ask yourself whether the address itself looks professional. We have seen so many which have been nicknames (often borderline inappropriate) and do not give the right impression. It is so easy to start a new email address; if in doubt, use an email address with your name in some format.

It may take several attempts to get your CV as you would want it but it is worth persevering. Bear in mind you may need several versions of your CV for the different job targets you are pursuing.

CVs for career changers

Career changers are typically unable to show experience in their target field and so relying on a CV to do the work for them is difficult. As you will have read in the networking section, most opportunities for career changers will be discovered by meeting people and proposing how you might be able to use your skills to add value to their organization.

For example, you can't hide the fact that you are a teacher and you now want to be a marketing manager, but what you can do is show very clearly your cross-transferable skills.

Some career specialists, and indeed some of our clients, have had success with functional CVs; this is when you state your cross-transferable skills as a heading and then list below the evidence of these skills. Sometimes this isn't possible as you may have had several jobs, in which case you may want to list your cross-transferable skills upfront and then provide a reverse chronological summary of your employment history. The downside of this approach is it makes it difficult for an employer to understand where in your employment history your cross-transferable skills were gained. We prefer a more upfront approach of listing your experience like a standard reverse chronological CV but clearly emphasizing your cross-transferable skills in each bullet point.

One key point for a career changer's CVs is to remove jargon. This is especially true if you are trying to change into a different industry or function, as you will need to make what you have done to date understandable to this new audience. Some organizations have a raft of in-house jargon which is not easily understandable and if you have been using it for a while you may not notice it any more, or if you are using specific technical language it can be difficult to be understood outside that field. If in doubt, give your CV to someone outside your industry and ask them whether it is clear what you do.

Chapter 37

Using social media to job search

Social media has taken on an increasingly important role in a job search. Here we cover how to manage your profile, your networks and your personal brand on those tools we feel are most useful so you can get the most from each of them as you undertake your job search. It is vital that you are aware of your online presence, ensuring that what potential employers can see is what you would want them to see. Google yourself and make sure you check several pages back. Does every mention of you reflect your personal brand and your best self? We know of one organization which found some worrying photographs and posts on the eleventh page of a Google search and, after further discussion, withdrew their job offer. What photos are you making public on your Facebook or Instagram feed? Will they raise any questions of 'fit' or 'business appropriate behaviour'? Just as you spend time on perfecting your CV, so it makes sense to ensure that all your social media presence is equally reflective of your best self from an employment perspective.

Twitter

Twitter can be a useful tool for following companies and industry leaders you are interested in. Often both companies and industry experts tell their followers about jobs that are available, but equally valuable is that you have the opportunity to stay current about the field you want to get into. This is very useful for interviews and helps you look knowledgeable and like an insider – crucial if you are looking to change career.

For example, if you were looking for a role in sustainability in the UK or US then someone you should follow would be Shannon Houde, @walkoflifecoach; she is a specialist in careers in this field and provides useful insight into the sector and will sometimes flag up jobs. You may find you can build a relationship with a contact on Twitter so that they will accept an email or LinkedIn request. You can do this by retweeting posts and commenting on their updates. Always be constructive with any comments, even if you don't agree – no one likes to feel attacked. In terms of your profile, make sure it is professional and you have included professional keywords in your bio.

LinkedIn

LinkedIn has emerged as a major tool in the job-seeker's toolbox; it is crucial for anyone who wants to develop their career as well as for businesses in terms of business development and networking. Social-Hire (www.social-hire.com) is a social media marketing agency for the recruitment industry; the experience of its founder, Tony Restell has consistently been that social media has emerged as a major channel for companies who want to recruit – both as a means of researching and approaching target candidates and as a means of attracting them. Its experience is that companies view social media recruitment as a relatively low-cost recruitment method when compared with other routes to market such as career fairs or recruitment agencies; also it is much easier for them to have a large reach and gain access to the candidates they need using this method. In addition Social-Hire has seen the power and reach of internal referral programmes considerably strengthened by their leveraging of social sites. Increasing numbers of companies have large internal recruitment teams and incentivize their employees to find new staff. The popularity of this direct route to hiring is likely to stem from the fact that staff are unlikely to recommend someone unless they know the quality of their work or feel confident they would be a good fit for the organization. Of course a firm also reduces recruitment costs by not using a recruitment agency. It is therefore important to expand your network at every opportunity, to increase the likelihood of being internally referred to a job by an employee of a firm you want to work for. So what does this mean for you? It means you need to have a strong social media profile to take advantage of the growing use of social media in hiring. It is particularly important to increase the size of your network and to optimize the wording of your profile.

LinkedIn's features do change, so rather than give you technical details of how to use the tools, we will concentrate on the bare minimum you need to have in place.

- Professional photograph – typically a professional headshot in business attire.
- Heading which represents you correctly – picking out your Unique Selling Points, e.g. you are multilingual or have specialized in a particular area.
- An achievement-based summary.
- Highlights of your achievements in career history.
- Brief outline of companies you have worked for, or if a large company, the division you worked in.
- LinkedIn url is edited to provide a simple link to your profile, which you can use in your email signature.

- You have joined groups which you are interested in, which will be useful for networking.
- You have linked to past colleagues, peers, suppliers, previous managers, university friends, school friends, family friends and family.
- You have signed up to follow companies and/or people you are interested in to gain sector knowledge.

Crucially you will want to make sure your profile has the words that recruiters are actually searching for (i.e. it's been keyword optimized). You can do this by searching on a job board for the typical types of role you would like to secure. Then ensure the words you see to describe what they are looking for are incorporated as much as possible into your profile. You still need your profile to read professionally and not like a jumbled list of keywords, but unless your profile has the words recruiters are actually using to search, you are unlikely to be found. If you want to be seen as an 'expert' in your field, LinkedIn provides the opportunity to blog via their platform. This means that your posts can be seen by all your contacts. Make sure that in 'settings' you have turned on your 'news mention' broadcasts. When following people you want to build a relationship with, you can comment and repost their content.

Other social media considerations

There are other social media sites where you can replicate the profile you have on LinkedIn. Google + is particularly worth considering because of the search capabilities of Google. Also it is worth filling in your Work History, Education, Professional Skills and Location on your Facebook profile as some employers will use Facebook to post job adverts targeted at specific groups of candidates. If you are in the creative industries, consider building a professional profile on more creative sites such as Instagram and YouTube. The best way to work out which social media sites you need to be on is to see where your target companies and key influencers have an active presence.

When you are updating your social media profile, make sure you 'turn off' your notifications so everyone in your network is not alerted when you change one word. Building your social media profile takes time and commitment; tools like Hootsuite and Buffer (they both have free versions) are very useful in scheduling communications to go out in advance. While writing original content is useful in building your credibility, curating existing content and then sharing is valuable in building your expertise. Finally, keep current! There are new avenues to social media constantly being introduced – ensure you are keeping up to date.

Chapter 38

Interviews

> I do the very best I know how – the very best I can; and I
> mean to keep on doing so until the end.
>
> *Abraham Lincoln*

If everything has gone to plan, your covering letter and CV
have been compelling and you have been invited in to meet
an interviewer. Unfortunately interviewing is not an exact
science. Very few people are ever trained to conduct interviews and you may come across someone who only talks
about themself and hardly asks you a question, or someone
who has a list of questions they want to get through but no
real sense of why they are asking them. It often helps if you
work on the basis that it is your job to do the interviewer's job
for them. If you know the skills and competencies they are
looking for, rather than waiting for the interviewer to enquire
about them, highlight them in your answers during your
time together. It is up to you to get your message across. Not
all interviews are about getting the job – early interviews may
be just to screen out unsuitable candidates or to reduce the
number of applicants to a manageable number to be introduced to the manager who will decide on who gets the job.
Knowing the purpose of your interview and what stage you
are at in the process can be useful to how you structure your
answers. Over the years we have seen interviewees fall into
some common traps that can count against them in their job
search. We have set out below some of those traps and some
interviewing etiquette in the hope that you can avoid them
and show yourself to be a prime candidate.

There are plenty of books on self-branding if you want some detailed advice about this area, but the key is to think carefully about how you present yourself. We have seen many younger people fall into the trap of not looking professional enough and older people who come across as old-fashioned and stuck in a time warp! How you look will affect how you feel about yourself and whether you radiate confidence. As a general rule we recommend you err on the side of dressing conservatively unless you are going to an interview in the creative industries. For women 'dressing for interview' is slightly trickier as they have to look professional but also 'up to date', perhaps wearing an accessory or two to show a little individuality. The most important thing is that you inspire confidence. Uncared-for nails or scruffy shoes do little to promote this image; it is more important that you are remembered for what you say rather than what you wore.

We may as well start with the obvious things. We have already covered this earlier in the book with informational interviews and it's the same for job interviews. Be on time. Getting there on time is vital – even being late because of traffic just doesn't cut it. And we know this is probably too much information, but if you use the bathroom before your interview, always wash your hands before you leave. Over the years, we have heard too many interviewers complain (particularly the men!) that they have just seen someone not wash their hands and they know that they are going to be the next to shake hands with them. The office reception has caught many a candidate out as they chat inappropriately on their mobile phone while being listened to by the interviewer. In reception you can learn quite a lot about a company. What is the vibe? Is it upbeat and positive? Do employees look happy and engaged or does everyone look like the grim reaper is just around the corner? Also this is a place people can learn about you, so take the time to be nice to the receptionist, as first impressions count.

First impressions

First impressions are incredibly important and in the first few seconds of meeting you, interviewers are making their mind up about you – just as you do, when you are introduced to someone new. It is important to try and be yourself as far as possible in interviews so that the interviewer can truly assess whether you will be a good fit in a particular role. If you are an introvert, don't try to come across as a party-loving extrovert. A recruiter is not only looking for someone with the right skills and experience for a role, they are also looking for a good match for the team or environment that the person will be joining. Although it may seem counter-intuitive, try to avoid having the mindset that it is more important to be offered the job than being offered the *right* job – you may end up kicking yourself if you find yourself in the wrong job in the wrong team.

Preparation before an interview is vital and will give you an edge – don't just have a quick look at the company's website (everyone will have done that). Who are their competitors? What did their most recent press release say? Is it relevant? What trends have you noticed in the industry? You might want to do a SWOT analysis (Strengths, Weaknesses, Opportunities and Threats) on the industry, company or their main product. Building rapport with the interviewer is always helpful – we are all human and if we like the person sitting opposite us, we are more likely to be well disposed towards them. How can you do that? Make eye contact – we find some people we interview will look almost anywhere other than at us! Smile, not all the time and use your common sense – smiling when you are talking about making a team redundant doesn't make sense; engage with the person you are with by smiling at appropriate times. Try and match their conversational style – if they are very to the point, try and match that and make your answers more succinct and clear. If they tend to tell more of a story when they are talking, try and do the same. Don't assume that the person interviewing you has read your CV or has been briefed on your abilities. It is important to create opportunities to sell yourself and highlight why you and your previous experience are key to the role. Don't presume that because it is on your CV they are aware that you are perfect for the job.

The interview is a two-way process. Having done all the hard work on establishing what you are looking for in your next role, bear this in mind when you are being interviewed. Is this really the role for you? Could you work in this environment? It is also important that you listen to the interviewer and show your interest by asking them questions that arise from their description of the role or about the company. You may well identify potential issues that they are facing which you have experience of tackling. It may seem obvious, but your attitude when you go into the interview will often determine the outcome. If you go into the interview with the belief you will be invited back for the next interview or offered the job, you are far more likely to be successful. If you think you are unlikely to get through, guess what ... you're probably right.

General questions

While you can't prepare for every question you are going to get asked, it is worth being prepared for some of the more common ones:

- Tell me about yourself/talk me through your CV
- Why are you applying?
- Why are you the best candidate for this role?
- Why do you want to leave your present employer?
- If I rang your boss for a reference, what would he or she say?
- Why would we hire you?
- How long will it take you to make a contribution?
- What interests do you have outside work?
- What has been your biggest achievement in your last role? In your life?
- What is your biggest weakness?
- What do you know about us?

One of the first questions you may get asked is: 'So, tell me about yourself.' This is your chance to sell yourself and deliver a clear, articulate, 'elevator' pitch. It is very easy to fall into the trap of being too long-winded, but an 'elevator' pitch is essentially your opportunity to talk about yourself in an engaging and positive way in the time it takes to go from the ground floor to the top floor in an elevator.

As with your CV, it is useful to start from your education and work your way forward in your career, explaining why you have made the decisions you have (why did you take your university course, go into a particular career, etc.). If you have seen an advert or specification for the job you are interviewing for, you will have a list of the core skills and competencies that are required. When you are talking about your career to date, try and highlight those skills and experience so you set the scene that you have what they are looking for. Remember to bring the recruiter right up to date and explain why you are looking for a new role and why you are particularly interested in this role.

List below what you think are your three Unique Selling Points (USPs) and practise weaving them into your elevator pitch:

1

2

3

You *will* get questions that are hard to answer. Bear in mind that sometimes the interviewer is interested in *how* you answer the questions when you don't know the answer as well as when you do! Can you think on your feet?

If there is a particular question that you really don't want to answer (e.g. why you didn't go to university, why you left a job, etc.), it is worth having an answer prepared that you are reasonably happy with. We usually find that when you are prepared, the question never arises, and when you're not, you can count on it making an appearance. We have also seen so many people start waffling when it comes to things they don't want to talk about and bizarrely they will then talk for far longer on the one thing they don't want to highlight on their CV. Be prepared and it will feel so much easier.

It is always the best policy to be honest but upbeat and positive. Most people dread the last question: 'What is your biggest weakness?' Be honest (recruiters get bored with stock answers such as 'I'm a perfectionist'!) but pick something that isn't a deal breaker; you don't want to totally rule yourself out of the job! Choose something you are working on or have improved recently. For example, this could be presentation skills which you could say you are actively working on and have recently joined a public speaking organization (as long as you have!) so you can regularly practise this skill.

Take some time to answer questions you find difficult – it is far better to take a few moments to gather your thoughts rather than rushing into giving an ill-thought-out answer or run the risk of giving an answer that goes on too long and is unstructured. You can buy some time by taking a breath, doing the 'thinking pose' (where you show in your facial expression that you are) or use filler phrases such as 'let me think about the best example of that'. We often get asked how long you should talk for when answering a question and as a general rule, between two and three minutes per answer is probably long enough. If your answer is necessarily longer, keep an eye on the interviewer and watch whether they are still with you – if in doubt, break the answer down into parts and ask if they have any questions. Avoid jargon and keep your answers clear and simple – getting too technical or going into too much detail can mean that your main points get lost.

Competency-based questions

Many companies, particularly large ones, recruit against competencies. We asked Elizabeth Bird, a recruitment specialist (www.indigogreenconsulting.com), what she would advise people as they prepare for these types of interview. Elizabeth has extensive experience in attracting, assessing and selecting graduate, MBA and experienced level hires for a variety of blue chip organizations including Arthur D. Little and Shell International, advising on recruitment techniques, interviewing skills and attracting the best talent. This is her advice:

Competency-based interviews (CBI) are prevalent in selection processes and yet, from my experience of conducting thousands, very few people are well prepared for them. For clarification, these are the types of interview which focus on questions that assess relevant competency for a role, for example:

- leadership
- communication skills
- teamwork

The premise of CBIs is that past behaviour is the best indicator of future behaviour (we tend to behave in similar ways in similar situations, unless we've had a strong intervention which changes that behaviour). The purpose of such an interview, then, is to elicit evidence from the candidate to understand how they have behaved during a specific event in the past in order to determine whether their behaviours align with the requirements of the job and the company culture and values. You can tell if a question is competency-based if it references your past – so it may start with the words, 'Tell me about a time when …' or 'Describe a situation when …'

There are two main reasons candidates fail a competency-based interview. First, the candidate (probably) does have the relevant experience, behaviours and values but chooses the wrong example to illustrate these. This may be because the candidate doesn't listen to the question or, worse, tries to shoehorn their 'prepared' example into whatever question is asked. Or the candidate hasn't considered *why* the question is being asked and what the interviewer is wanting from an answer. As a consequence, they talk about an example which lacks depth, at best, and is probably irrelevant.

Secondly (and very frustratingly for the interviewer), the candidate does have the relevant experience and a potentially excellent example, but struggles to externalize the information appropriately. This is the candidate who loses focus, talks too much and provides too much immaterial information. This is also the candidate who undersells their contribution, failing to recognize the value of their input and express what they did and, very importantly, *how* they did it.

My advice regarding preparing for interview as a candidate is to start by knowing yourself, your skills, how you have behaved in specific situations and what value you bring. Only then will you be able to articulate your value and behaviours in a clear and structured way.

Over the years of interviewing candidates at all levels, certain trends have emerged regarding why candidates are not successful during competency-based interviews. Here are my recommended Do's and Don't's for behavioural competency interviews:

Do ...

- Prepare behavioural competency examples
- Listen to the question (ask for it to be repeated or rephrased if necessary)
- Take time to think before answering a question
- Consider why the question has been asked and select the most appropriate example
- Talk about your own personal contribution and how you behaved
- Use the opportunities provided to 'sell' yourself into the role – make sure you don't underplay what you did

Don't ...

- Provide vague and non-specific answers
- Talk too much and provide irrelevant information

- Make up or exaggerate examples (a strong interviewer will uncover this!)
- Talk about 'we' (the focus should be on 'I' during behavioural competency interviews)

We have found that the **STAR(R)** format is very effective in giving a complete answer to these types of question, which is why we have used this format in the Skills Exercise in Part II.

S – What **situation** was this?
T – What was the **task** you had to perform?
A – What was the **action** that you took?
R – What was the **result** that you got?
(R) – With certain answers, it can also be useful to **reflect** on what you learned in the situation or talk about the **relationships** you dealt with.

Some competencies are specific to the role and some to the company. A recruiter is likely to have a list of these competencies which he/she will work through in the interview, trying to gather evidence for each one. The job specification often details the competencies being sought for the role. Sometimes company-specific competencies can be found on the company's website, for example in a list of 'core values' or in a mission statement. Once you have an idea of the competencies you will need to demonstrate, refer back to the results of the skills exercise in Part II. Decide which examples would best demonstrate the competencies you think they might be looking for. The knowledge you gain about yourself from the exercise will make it much easier to answer even the most unlikely competency-based questions.

Strength-based interviews

One type of interview you might come across, particularly at graduate level, is the strength-based interview. We are also increasingly seeing this type of interview used at a more senior level. It is a type of interview that benefits the candidate too, as the questions are designed to find out what you love to do and do well – to make sure you'll enjoy the job, perform well and fit in with the organization. Its origins come from companies realizing that those who enjoy what they do are more likely to perform better and be more productive at work. Employers like it as it is harder to prepare for and they are less likely to get standardized answers. However you still need to prepare. You can do this by considering how your preferences fit with the type of work on offer and the organization's values. The exercises you did in the first half of the book are very important in giving you this evidence. These answers are more difficult to fake, as your body language or inconsistencies in your answers may give you away. Be aware that when you are asked what you don't like doing, this will naturally lead into your weaknesses, so be careful how you frame them.

Here are some examples of strength-based questions you might get asked:

- What work do you find easy?
- What work do you find difficult?
- What would you say is your biggest achievement, and how did you do it?
- What would you say a successful day looks like?
- What were your favourite subjects at school?
- What activities give you energy?
- How would a close friend describe you to a stranger?
- What do you like to do in your spare time?

Try and go into the interview as relaxed as possible and be yourself. If you get rejected then it's very likely that the role and the organization wasn't a good fit anyway.

Questions for you to ask

Crucially, as we stated in Part III, the questions you ask at interview are a strong indication of how much research you have done on the company and now seriously you are taking the interview. Don't ask questions which can be answered from the internet but find ones that are more subjective.

Example questions are:

- Why is the job open?
- Why did you join this company?
- What would my first assignment be?
- What are the development plans for the role/department?
- In your opinion, who will be the company's competitors in the future?
- Who will I be reporting to?

If you are at the beginning of the interview process (most companies will do more than one interview to recruit for a role), ask questions that will give you additional insight to build upon at subsequent interviews. This will give you an edge over other applicants as you will appear more knowledgeable.

Tammy was a recruiter at an investment bank and says the questions the applicants asked at the end of the interview process were as important as the questions they answered during it, as it demonstrated the level of research a candidate had gone to and whether they were serious about the company and the position.

Common interview mistakes

We find that the same mistakes crop up again and again. The main ones are:

- Not having done enough research on the company or industry as a whole. This shows a lack of interest and enthusiasm.
- Not listening to the question or answering a question you wish the interviewer had asked. This may work for politicians but won't work at interview.
- Providing too much information. Try and make sure that the information you are giving is relevant, succinct and to the point while still highlighting the important pieces of the story.
- Negotiating your salary before you've been offered the job.
- Criticizing your current or previous employer.
- Focusing only on what you will get out of the role (promotion, higher salary, etc.) – the focus should be on what you can do for the company.
- Highlighting negatives when the question hasn't asked for it.

Assessment centres

Assessment centres are usually used to test and observe groups of candidates to see if they match the requirements of the role(s) being recruited for. They are usually run by experienced professionals who do this regularly and you will usually be briefed in advance on what to expect. Interviews, personality questionnaires, group exercises, individual presentations, role plays and in-box exercises (which require a candidate to show how they would deal with typical items in an in-box/in-tray and are used to assess how they would prioritize, plan, delegate and deal with correspondence, memos, etc.) as well as numerical and verbal reasoning tests, are the main selection tools used at assessment centres. You can't really practise for group exercises and personality tests. It is better just to be yourself and to try not to second guess what they want. You can practise for numerical and verbal reasoning tests, giving yourself a better chance of a higher score on the day. If you are keen to do some practice, you can often find numerical and verbal reasoning tests at university careers centres that will have samples online. If you have an MBA you can revisit the work done in preparing for the GMAT test. These tests are very similar in content to the management level tests you are likely to encounter. Test publishers often have sample tests you can complete to help you build your confidence and get some practice – for example, SHL has a useful site at https://www.cebglobal.com/shldirect/en/practice-tests/

When it comes to the other exercises during an assessment centre, be yourself – you want to be assessed on who you are, not on who you think you should be.

Top ten common pitfalls at an assessment centre

We asked a group of assessment centre experts to share the mistakes they see frequently:

1 **Overlooking important information in the joining instructions**
   Remember to bring all relevant documentation with you to the assessment centre; it saves everyone time and

aggravation if you come along with the right paperwork on the day and makes a good first impression. For example, you may be asked to bring a copy of your passport and receipts for travel expenses. Also, don't forget to check whether you need to do any pre-work in preparation for the day.

2 **Arriving late**
What does it say about your ability to organize yourself in a job if you are late for the start of the assessment? Plan your journey and make sure that you allow plenty of time to get to the venue.

3 **Worrying excessively about your performance**
Assessors want to see you as you typically behave and will do whatever they can to help you relax and enjoy the experience so that they can observe the 'real you'. Try to engage fully in all the assessment activities and take on roles that come naturally to you. For example, in a group exercise, candidates often volunteer to take notes or write on the flip chart so they are 'doing something', without realizing that potentially this removes them from discussion or engaging with the group. Only offer to take on this role if you have the ability to use this opportunity to help shape or facilitate the discussion.

4 **Forgetting to behave appropriately outside the set assessment centre exercises**
Remember you are potentially being observed at any time during the course of the assessment. Pay attention to what you talk about in down time in the interests of building rapport and always question how appropriate your topic of conversation might be. Try to engage with the other candidates and avoid being selective about who you engage with.

5   **Making negative comments about the process and the simulations**

It potentially shows a certain naivety if you openly criticize the process when the assessors will be evaluating your performance. It is likely that you will be asked to evaluate the assessment centre process at the end of the day, which is your opportunity to constructively critique your experience.

6   **Skim reading the exercise instructions**

Candidates who pay scant attention to the instructions for any exercise tend to miss important details and perform less effectively than others. It is easy to get distracted at an assessment centre, but please remember to read through exercise instructions carefully.

7   **Under-utilizing the exercise preparation time**

Assessors frequently walk into a role play or presentation and candidates will still be making notes or annotating flip charts. This suggests they have not taken the instructions as literally as they would in the real world and then expect extra time to finish off their preparation. In a real world situation, if your boss had asked for a presentation for a client within one hour, you would not dream of asking your boss and the client to wait a few minutes as they walk into the room; you would make absolutely sure that you are ready to present.

8   **Second guessing the assessment centre process**

Candidates will occasionally try to be too clever by trying to guess what the assessors want to see – for example, assuming they are looking for a leader when they are more likely to be looking for a team player. This can be a big mistake as you will typically act out of character and not fully immerse yourself in the situation. Second guessing the process limits your ability to perform well and in reality you are very likely to have got all or some of it wrong. The smart approach is just to do what you are asked in the instructions.

9 'Performing' for the assessors
   Remember you are not on *The Apprentice*! A trap that candidates frequently fall into is to 'perform' for the assessors. For example, in a group exercise, you may look for the assessor who you think is assessing you and put on a performance for them. Assessors frequently observe candidates who deliver their contributions as much to them as to the rest of the group. This is unlikely to enhance your performance potential. Remember that a group exercise is designed to assess how effectively you engage in a task as part of a team.

10 Deferring action in an assessment exercise
    If the exercise instructions ask you to deal with an issue, this is because the assessors want to see you deal with the issue. Many candidates choose to discuss it a bit, superficially, but then suggest meeting at a later date, which obviously isn't going to happen. Assessors can't use evidence from a hypothetical future conversation, so please take the opportunity to demonstrate what you can do for maximum performance benefit.

Panel interviews

Occasionally you may face several interviewers (usually three or four) at once. This is particularly common in interviews for the public sector and you will usually be told that this is the case prior to the interview. If this is the first time you have faced a panel it can be daunting, but everyone is in the same boat. While addressing your answer to the person who asked the question, it is important to include the whole panel of interviewers in your answer, by glancing at them while you are answering the questions to make them feel included, as if you were telling a story to your friends but trying to impress one person the most!

You may get one of the interviewers asking really tough questions and one asking easy ones – this good guy/bad guy routine is designed to ruffle your feathers. Try and stay calm. Remember that you were asked to the interview because they thought you were a strong candidate for the job otherwise they wouldn't have wasted your time or theirs – they are doing the same to all the candidates.

Telephone interviews

More and more interviews are now conducted initially by telephone to save on cost and time. We recommend the following:

- If possible, make sure you are on a landline in a quiet place to ensure no problems with reception or distractions of background noise.
- Vary the tone and pace of your voice to add interest.
- Tell the interviewer if you need some time to think through an answer. As before, phrases such as 'Let me think of the best example of that' are good filler phrases that buy you some time to think.
- Some candidates find standing up gives their voice more gravitas or talking in front of a mirror. It sounds a little odd but it really can work!

Follow-up letters

The smallest act of kindness is worth more than the grandest intention.

Oscar Wilde

After any meeting we recommend you write a short follow-up letter, but after an interview it is particularly powerful. This letter can reiterate why you think you are the right person for the job. Often after a meeting you can think 'I wish I'd said that' or 'I wonder if they are concerned about this or that'. By writing a follow-up letter you give yourself the chance to reflect and address these issues. It shows you are interested in the job and gives the impression that you will be professional in following up with clients. Keeping in touch with the company even if you aren't successful is a good way to stay on their radar, as their first choice may turn down the role, not work out, or – as in Louise's case – a new opportunity opens up within the company.

Louise signed up for job alerts from Guardian Jobs (online). This led her to apply for a position with a children's charity in its North regional office in Leeds. She wasn't offered the role but received positive feedback and was asked to stay in touch. She also signed up to several recruitment agencies in the not for profit sector. One of them contacted her to say that a job suitable for her was being advertised in the North West. It turned out to be the same job title/description she had applied for previously but from a different regional office of the children's charity. She thanked the recruiter but let them know that as she had previously applied to the charity direct, she couldn't let the recruiter work on her application from an ethical point of view. She then emailed the Head of Region in the North (Leeds) who had already interviewed her and asked whether, if appropriate, she could refer her to the Head of Region in the North West (Manchester), which she did. And after another two rounds of interviews she got the job ... So staying in touch and persistence worked.

Rejection

It is impossible to live without failing at something, unless you live so cautiously that you might as well not have lived at all, in which case you have failed by default.

JK Rowling, Harvard Commencement Speech –
© JK Rowling 2008

Rejection is a component of the job search process and there is no getting away from it. We often find that a candidate will have put all their focus on one role and if they get rejected, find it hard to get motivated to start from scratch again. For that reason, we recommend that you have at least ten opportunities that you are interested in (e.g. you have applied for the role) and aim for five opportunities that seem promising (e.g. you are at interview stage). So often, many of these opportunities will disappear through no fault of your own: the company has decided not to recruit after all, an internal candidate has been selected, and so on. If you have more options on the go, although you may be disappointed, you will have more positive avenues to pursue, which can lessen the rollercoaster effect.

There is also an upside that most people don't consider. The interviewer may well have thought that your experience and skill set were the best but felt you would not fit into the team; they may well have saved you from a role you would have hated – so perhaps a rejection can be a blessing in disguise. If you do want to learn from the experience, you can contact the interviewer to ask for feedback. Be friendly and polite but don't push. Often they won't be able to give you useful feedback: it was a close-run thing and they just felt the other candidate was a better fit; there was nothing you could have done better. A positive mindset is vital, especially after being turned down for a job. Watch the language you use – not 'I'm not working', rather 'I am considering several career options at the moment'. Mental health or state of mind is crucial when job hunting (and in life generally!). When you feel low and lack confidence you'll have worse days than when you feel confident and buoyant! Job hunting can be tough and so can changing career, but you are not alone, so try to keep a sense of perspective. You can't work on your career or job hunt 24/7 – taking time off can make you more fired up when you return and you will appear more relaxed and less 'manic' at interview.

Chapter 39

Negotiating the job and the salary

Fortune favours the bold.

Proverb

It's always a good idea to negotiate the job first and the salary second. If all goes well, you will start to receive job offers. Early on in the recruitment process we suggest you are vague about your salary requirements by giving a broad-brush figure. If you are pushed into stating a salary, a good response is 'I'm looking for the market rate for this type of job', or depending on how much knowledge you have, you could say 'until I know more about the role it is difficult to know'. If you are asked directly for the figure that you earn now, then you will have to give one. Don't forget to add in all the benefits you receive as this can inflate the overall figure. If you are due a salary review soon you can also take this into account but disclose this to your interviewer. If you feel your salary doesn't reflect what you are worth now – perhaps you have just invested in an MBA, for example – the best way to negotiate the salary is to focus on how well you meet the requirements and what value you can add to the company.

Try to generate as many job opportunities as possible – you are likely to come across as more confident at interview if you have options. If you are desperate because this job interview is the only one you have, that is hard to hide. It also weakens your position. Giving the impression you are actively on the market with several options open identifies you as a good candidate, meaning it is far more likely you will be offered a salary commensurate with the position. It's a game and if a company thinks that this is your only option, they may be tempted to come in with a low salary. If they get the impression you have some other serious options, the company is more likely not to 'push it's luck' and offer a higher salary to secure you.

Getting the timing right

We recommend that you don't start to negotiate the salary until you have had an offer from the company, ideally in writing. If you state a salary that is too low or too high you can put yourself out of the game without discussing and negotiating the job.

If the offer is below the market level you either need to renegotiate the job, because if the job content changes the more likely the salary level can be negotiated, or you can negotiate what you feel is a fairer market rate. You should be able to find out what the market rate is by asking recruitment agencies, looking at job advertisements, studying salary studies in professional journals and making some discreet enquiries in your network – asking contacts for salary bands. Sites like www.glassdoor.com can be useful too. Basic salary is not the only area you can negotiate on, you may be able to negotiate on the benefits or perhaps more regular salary reviews. We have had clients negotiate an equity stake in a company as a way to get round a lower initial starting salary in a start-up company. Others have decided they would prefer to negotiate their working week by a day or include executive coaching in their salary package. Of course this all depends on the currency of your skills in the market place and the economic climate, which is why it is a good idea to regularly assess your worth within your industry.

Fiona interviewed for an IT senior role within a bank. She was over-qualified for the role but the bank offered her the salary for this role anyway. Fiona asked for another meeting with the decision makers (the IT Director and the CEO) and renegotiated the role to include more responsibility, which she clearly had the experience to deliver. Given the increased remit of the role, when Fiona asked for a much increased salary, the company agreed and effectively created a new role for her at 20 per cent more than the salary they offered her initially.

Chapter 40

The first 100 days

> Start by doing what's necessary; then do what's possible; and suddenly you are doing the impossible.
>
> *St Francis of Assisi*

When you start in a new job, you are going to go through a considerable amount of change, which begins when you accept the job offer and usually continues until about three months after you've started the new role.

Having an action plan to hit the ground running can considerably ease that period of change. You will never have a second chance to make a first impression, so here are some aspects of a new role you may want to think about at key stages to make the best of your first three months.

Before you start

- Is there any additional research you can do about the company, their clients, your close colleagues and the industry that would be helpful prior to joining?
- How do you want to be perceived in the new business?
- Do you know how the company/your new boss is going to assess how well you are settling into your new role?

First month

- Do you have a clear understanding of reporting lines and

the expectations your new boss/the company has for you? Are they achievable?

- Is the job as you expected or do you need to re-evaluate how you approach it?
- Do you have an action plan for the first three months? What do you want to achieve? How do you want to be perceived?
- What 'early wins' can you work on to show your value to the company?
- Depending on your level of seniority, do you know the company strategy?
- Are there any influential people you have met who might act as mentors as you embed yourself in the company?
- When you first start, watching, listening and learning can be very useful as a strategy. Who are the real decision makers? What is the culture like, both formal and informal? Whose opinions count most in decision making?
- Don't be tempted to respond to negative comments from new colleagues. Find out the lie of the land before you weigh in with your opinion.

Third month

- Is the role progressing as expected? If not, what can you do to get it back on track?
- Do you have an action plan for the rest of the year?
- When will your performance be assessed? Do you know what you are being assessed against? Are there any areas you need to work on to ensure that the assessment is beyond expectations?

The important thing to remember is that getting the job is not where the career strategy ends. The most successful individuals are constantly looking at how they can deliver better and develop faster than their peers. You can do the same.

Chapter 41

Long-term career management

> If you don't have a plan for yourself, you'll be part of someone else's.
>
> *American proverb*

You can't tell what will happen in the future, and we all have to be flexible to changing circumstances. Knowing yourself and what you want goes a long way to carving out a satisfying and successful career. Having this knowledge helps you avoid career cul-de-sacs and recognize opportunities when you see them.

One of the biggest changes in the job market in the last twenty-five years is that the concept of a job for life is becoming increasingly rare. There is an expectation that people will now manage their own careers, looking for opportunities to develop with a plan of what they want to achieve and where they want to go in terms of their work life. In reality, most people drift into a career almost by default – a comment from a teacher, parent, family friend who suggests that a certain job might suit their skills – and then find themselves on a conveyor belt that involves a promotion, the occasional new job when either they are forced to move (redundancy) or feel they need a change or salary rise. Usually very little strategic thinking goes into those decisions or whether the direction in which they are moving and that felt was right early in their career is now appropriate. What we hope is that this book will encourage you to become more strategic about your own career.

From the moment you start earning your own living, you are effectively running your own consultancy company with one, very important, employee: you. You will need to have a strategy that responds to the market changes, your values, your needs (financial and otherwise). As any good company would do, we suggest you review this on a regular basis, thinking of your employers as your consultancy clients. You are there to do a piece of consultancy for them; when you or they feel that that value has passed, you move on.

Annual career health check

Each year, we suggest you do a quick review of where you are to ensure you are on track towards your long-term career goals:

- What have you learned in the last year?
- How have you progressed since your last career health check?
- How have you extended your network?
- How have you contributed to your team/organization?
- How is your current role now aligned with your long-term career goals?
- What are your key goals for the coming year?

Key impacts on your long-term career management strategy

As you navigate your career and keep an eye on where your industry/career is going in the future, you should consider:

1   **New employment trends – keep an eye on where your**

industry/career is going in the future so you can consider this as you navigate your career.

2   Keeping your skills up to date – it is important to consider what training you need to get to the next level in your career.

3   Your changing circumstances – whether intentional or inadvertent, there is one thing you can count on: your life will change.

4   Can you find a new mentor and/or sponsor who can help you progress and give you guidance? It can be useful to have perspectives from respected senior colleagues or contacts outside the usual corporate appraisal system.

5   Is it possible to create new opportunities in your current organization or is it time for a fresh start?

It is well worth reviewing your matrix once a year to see if what you are looking for in a role/career is still the same or if your requirements are changing. Perhaps you now have children and work/life balance is more of a priority, or global travel is not quite the draw it once was. After completing this process, you may feel it is time to move on. Perhaps the 'cons' of the role now outweigh the 'pros', or you may feel your career has now stalled. We hope that if you feel you have gone as far as you can, you will turn to the exercises in the book and start planning the future. Make it a positive experience – moving confidently towards the future rather than negatively away from the past.

Chapter 42

Final thoughts

> The only real failure in life is not to be true to the best one knows.
>
> *Buddha*

Having been through this process and then helped our clients navigate this methodology, we are keen to share what we have learnt both as recruiters and as career coaches. Many people find the process hard work and some will not put in sufficient effort to reap the rewards, but we hope we have done enough through the book and with the case studies to show just what is possible if you keep going, even when it gets tough. The rewards really are worth the effort.

Without a doubt this process takes time and effort but, as our clients testify, it is worth it to have a career that you are engaged with and enjoy. You can tell at interview those candidates who have a real passion and interest in their work; their eyes shine and they have more energy. We believe life is too precious not to make the most of your working life and we have given you in this book everything we have learnt, both about ourselves and through our clients, about how to navigate your career.

This is the book that we wish we had both had when we started trying to carve a more satisfying career. The idea of writing it came about when we were discussing what we would like to achieve in the year that would stretch us, achieve a long-held goal and strengthen our own careers – i.e. career strategizing! We were lucky enough, through networking, to find a publisher who liked what we had to say (thank you Emily and the Bloomsbury team!).

We hope, as you work your way through the book, that you discover options and we encourage you to make a start on taking a proactive approach to your career. We hope, too, that the stories of our clients will inspire you to fulfil your potential in work and life generally – enjoy the journey!

References and Resources

Often books have very large reference and resource sections and you are left no wiser as to which book or resource to choose out of a very long list. We would rather guide you to the books we know we and our clients have found particularly helpful rather than just giving you an Amazon search list. We have chosen our references and resources sparingly, to focus on what we feel will be the most useful for you.

Part I: The career change process

Time management

Allen, David (2015) *Getting Things Done: The Art of Stress-free Productivity*. Piatkus

Tracey, Brian (2013) *Eat That Frog! Get More of the Important Things Done – Today!* Hodder Paperbacks

Overcoming fear

Goddard, Gabriella (2006) *Gulp!: The Seven-day Crash Course to Master Fear and Break Through Any Challenge*. Penguin

Jeffers, Susan (2007) *Feel The Fear and Do It Anyway*. Vermilion

Johnson, Spencer, Dr (1999) *Who Moved My Cheese? An Amazing Way to Deal with Change in Your Work and in Your Life*. Vermillion

Part II: Understanding yourself and what you want

Career tests

Passmore, Jonathan (2008) *Psychometrics in Coaching: Using Psychological and Psychometric Tools for Development*. Kogan Page

Tieger D. Paul and Barbara Barron (2007) *Do What You Are: Discover the Perfect Career for You Through the Secrets of Personality Type*. Little, Brown and Company

www.psychtesting.org.uk/directories – for a complete listing of practitioners listed by the BPS

www.intestcom.org – information about psychometric tests between countries

www.assessmentday.co.uk – a series of practice tests encompassing verbal and numerical reasoning and psychometric tests

Defining your skills and strengths

Buckingham Marcus and Clifton Donald (2013) *Now Discover Your Strengths*. Gallup Press

Rath, Tom (2007) *Strengthsfinder 2.0: A New and Upgraded Edition of the Online Test from Gallup's Now Discover Your Strengths*. Gallup Press

Your interests and passions

Sher, Barbara (2007) *Refuse to Choose!: Use All of Your Interests, Passions, and Hobbies to Create the Life and Career of Your Dreams*. Rodale Books

Robinson, Sir Ken (2014), *Finding Your Element: How to Discover Your Talents and Passions and Transform Your Life*. Penguin Books

Defining your long-term plan

Canfield, Jack (2007) *How to Get from Where You Are to Where You Want to Be*. Harper Element

Turner, Colin (2002) *Born to Succeed: Releasing Your Business Potential*. Texere Publishing

Part III: Now what? How to research, brainstorm and move forward

Research

Ibarra, Herminia (2013) *Working Identity: Unconventional Strategies for Reinventing Your Career*. Harvard Business School Press

These are websites you might find useful as you start researching sectors and functions:

www.careersbox.co.uk

www.glassdoor.com

www.vault.com

Setting up a business

Cantwell, Marianne (2013) *Be a Freerange Human, Escape the 9 to 5, Create a Life you Love and Still Pay the Bills*. Kogan Page

Gerber, Michael E. (1994) *E-Myth Revisited: Why Most Small Businesses Don't Work and What to Do About It*. HarperCollins

Hyatt, Michael (2012) *Platform: Get Noticed in a Noisy World – a Step-by-Step Guide for Anyone with Something to Say or Sell*. Thomas Nelson

Part IV: Practicalities of job applications

Networking

Carnegie, Dale (2007) *How to Win Friends and Influence People*. Vermilion

Sole, David and Belinda Roberts (2015) *21st-Century Networking: How to Become a Natural Networker*. Elliott & Thompson

Grant, Adam (2014) *Give and Take: Why Helping Others Drives Our Success*. W&N

King, Zella and Amanda Scott (2014) *Who is in Your Personal Boardroom? How to Choose People, Assign Roles and Have Conversations with Purpose*. CreateSpace Independent Publishing Platform

Townsend, Heather (2014) *The Financial Times Guide to Business Networking: How to use the power of online and offline networking for business and personal success*

Job search strategy

Dalton, Steve (2012) *The 2 Hour Job Search: Using Technology to Get the Right Job Faster*. Ten Speed Press

Influencing

Cialdini, Robert (2007) *Influence: The Psychology of Persuasion*. HarperBusiness

CVs

Mills, Corinne (2015) *You're Hired! How To Write a Brilliant CV*. Trotman

Howard, Simon (1999) *Creating a Successful CV*. Dorling Kindersley Limited

Covering letters
Innes, James (2009) *Brilliant Cover Letters: What You Need to Know to Write a Truly Brilliant Cover Letter*. Prentice Hall

Interviews
Porot, Daniel and Frances Bolles Haynes (2008) *Best Answers to 202 Job Interview Questions*. Impact Publications
Reed, James (2015) *Why You? 101 Interview Questions You'll Never Fear Again*. Portfolio Penguin
Yate, Martin John (2008) *Great Answers to Tough Interview Questions*. Kogan Page
Salary information and recruitment trends:
www.hays.co.uk/salary-guides
www.glassdoor.com

Portfolio working
Hopson, Barrie and Katie Ledger (2009) *And What Do You Do?: 10 Steps to Creating a Portfolio Career*. A&C Black

First 100 days
Watkins, Michael (2003) *The First 90 Days: Critical Success Strategies for New Leaders at All Levels*. Harvard Business School Press

Our Website

www.howtotakechargeofyourcareer.com
Here we link to more books we have found useful but are specific to a certain topic. It is also where we will flag up additional books that might be useful to readers.

The website is also where you can find downloadable blank forms for the exercises in this book.

Bibliography

Ball, Ben (1996) *Assessing Your Career: Time for Change? (Personal and Professional Development)*. London: Wiley Blackwell

Beckel, Heather (2002) *Be a Kickass Assistant: How to Get from a Grunt Job to a Great Career*. London: Headline

Black, Roger (1987) *Getting Things Done: A Radical New Approach to Managing Time and Achieving More at Work*. London: Penguin Group

Boldt, Laurence G. (1996) *How to Find the Work You Love*. London: Arkana

Bolles, Richard Nelson (2009a) *What Color is Your Parachute? 2010: A Practical Manual for Job-hunters and Career-changers*. London: Ten Speed Press

Bolles, Richard Nelson (2009b) *The Job-hunter's Survival Guide: How to Find Hope and Rewarding Work even when 'There are No Jobs'*. London: Ten Speed Press

Bolles, Richard Nelson and Howard Figler (1999) *The Career Counselor's Handbook*. London: Ten Speed Press

Bronson, Po (2004) *What Should I Do With My Life?* London: Vintage

Carson, Richard D. (2003) *Taming Your Gremlin (Revised): A Surprisingly Simple Method for Getting Out of Your Own Way*. San Francisco: HarperSanFrancisco

Chan, James (2000) *Spare Room Tycoon: Succeeding Independently – The 70 Lessons of Sane Self-employment*. London: Nicholas Brealey Publishing

Christensen, Clayton M., James Allworth and Karen Dillon (2012) *How Will You Measure Your Life? Finding Fulfilment Using Lessons From Some of the World's Greatest Businesses*. HarperCollins

Coomber, Stephen, Stuart Crainer and Des Dearlove (2002) *The Career Adventurer's Fieldbook: Your Guide to Career Success.* London: Capstone Publishing Limited

Cowper, William (1785) *The Task.* Joseph Jordan

De Grunwald, Tanya (2008) *Dude, Where's My Career? The Guide for Baffled Graduates.* West Sussex: Summersdale Publishers

Ducker, Chris (2014) *Virtual Freedom, How to Work with Virtual Staff to Buy More Time, Become More Productive and Build Your Dream Business.* Benbella Books, Inc

Ferris, Tim (2011) *The 4 Hour Work Week.* Vermilion

Flynn, Pat (2016) *Will it Fly? How to Test Your Next Business Idea So You Don't Waste Your Time and Money.* Flynn Industries LLC

Green, Graham (2008) *The Career Change Handbook: How to Find Out What You're Good At and Enjoy – Then Get Someone to Pay You For It.* Oxford: How To Books Ltd

Grigg, Joanna (1999) *Getting Into Self Employment.* London: Trotman & Co. Ltd

Guerriero, Janice M. and Robert G. Allen (1998) *Questions in Career Counselling – Techniques to Deliver Effective Career Counselling Services.* Philadelphia: Lawrence Erlbaum Associates Inc.

Hall, Richard (2008) *The Secrets of Success at Work: 10 Steps to Accelerating Your Career.* London: Pearson Education Limited

Handy, Charles B. and Elizabeth Handy (2004) *The New Alchemists.* London: Hutchinson

Hawkins, Dr Peter (1999) *The Art of Building Windmills: Career Tactics for the 21st Century.* Liverpool: Graduate Into Employment Unit

Heath, Chip and Dan (2013) *How to Make Better Choices in Life and Work.* Random House

Hopson, Barrie and Mike Scally (2009) *Build Your Own*

Rainbow: A Workbook for Career and Life Management. East Sussex: Management Books

Hornby, Malcolm (2000) *3 Easy Steps to the Job You Want.* London: Financial Times/Prentice Hall

Jacobs, Richard (2004) *What's Your Purpose? Seven Questions to Find Your Answer.* London: Mobius

Katz, Margot (2007) *Tarzan and Jane: How to Thrive in the New Corporate Jungle.* London: Profile

Keller, Gary with Papasan, Jay (2014) *The One Thing.* John Murray Learning

Klein, Steve (2000) *Jobwise: 150 Tips to Help You Survive and Thrive in Your Career.* London: John Wiley & Sons

Lees, John (2008) *How to Get a Job You'll Love: A Practical Guide to Unlocking Your Talents and Finding Your Ideal Career.* Berkshire: McGraw-Hill Professional

Lore, Nicholas (1998) *The Pathfinder: How to Choose or Change your Career for a Lifetime of Satisfaction and Success.* London: Simon & Schuster

Marshall, Judi (1995) *Women Managers Moving On: Exploring Career and Life Choices.* London: Thomson Learning

Messmer, Max (2000) *Managing Your Career for Dummies.* London: IDG Books Worldwide Inc.

Mrs Moneypenny with Heather McGregor (2013) *Mrs Moneypenny's Career Advice for Ambitious Women.* Porfolio Penguin

Nathan, Robert and Linda Hill (estate) (2005) *Career Counselling* (Counselling in Practice series). London: Sage

Nemko, Marty, Paul Edwards and Sarah Edwards (1998) *Cool Careers for Dummies.* London: IDG Books Worldwide Inc.

Oates, David and V. J. Shackleton (1994) *Perfect Recruitment: All You Need to Get it Right First Time.* London: Arrow Books Ltd

Otterbourg, Robert K. (2001) *Switching Careers.* Washington: The Kiplinger Washington Editors

Porot, Daniel (1996) *The Pie Method for Career Success; A Unique Way to Find Your Ideal Job*. Minneapolis: JIST Works Inc

Pink, Daniel H. (2008) *The Adventures of Johnny Bunko: The Last Career Guide You'll Ever Need*. New York: Business Plan

Prince, Jeffrey P. and Lisa J. Heiser (2000) *Essentials of Career Interest Assessment* (Essentials of Psychological Assessment). London: John Wiley & Sons

Pryce-Jones, Jessica (2010) *Happiness at Work: Maximising Your Psychological Capital for Success*. London: Wiley-Blackwell

Pyke, Gary and Neath, Stuart (2002) *Be Your Own Career Consultant: Where Do You Want To Be?* London: Pearson Education Limited

Robinson, Jonathan and Carmel McConnell (2002) *Un-Ltd: Tell Me What Is It You Plan To Do with Your One Wild and Precious Life*. London: Momentum

Rowe, Dorothy (1996) *The Successful Self*. London: HarperCollins

Shell, G. Richard (2013) *Springboard: Launching Your Personal Search for Success*. Portfolio Penguin

Sher, Barbara and Barbara Smith (1994) *I Could Do Anything If I Only Knew What It Was: How to Discover What You Really Want and How to Get It*. London: Bantam Doubleday Dell Publishing Group

Sisson, Natalie (2013) *The Suitcase Entrepreneur*. Tonawhai Press

Spillane, Mary (2000) *Branding Yourself: How to Look, Sound and Behave Your Way to Success*. London: Sidgwick & Jackson

Taylor, David (2002) *The Naked Leader*. London: Capstone

Taylor, Denise (2009) *How to Get a Job in a Recession*. Canada: Brook House Press

Taylor, Ros and John Humphrey (2001) *Fast Track to the Top: 10 Skills for Career Success*. London: Kogan Page Ltd

The Mind Gym (2006) *Give Me Time*. London: Time Warner Books

Tolle, Eckhart (2001) *The Power of Now: A Guide to Spiritual Enlightenment and Proven Strategies for Getting a Job You Love*. London: Marshall Cavendish

Waldroop, James and Timothy Butler (2001) *The 12 Bad Habits that Hold Good People Back: Overcoming the Behavior Patterns that Keep You from Getting Ahead*. London: Broadway Business

Wendleton, Kate (1999) *Interviewing and Salary Negotiation: For Job Hunters, Career Changers, Consultants and Freelancers*. New Jersey: The Career Press

White, Kate (1995) *Why Good Girls Don't Get Ahead but Gutsy Girls Do: Nine Secrets Every Career Woman Must Know*. New York: Grand Central Publishing

Williams, Nick (2000) *The Work We Were Born To Do: Find the Work You Love, Love the Work You Do*. London: Element Books

Winter, Barbara (1993) *Making a Living Without a Job: Winning Ways for Creating Work that You Love*. London: Bantam Books

Wright, Bridget (1999) *Careershift: How to Plan and Develop a Successful Career*. London: Piatkus Books

Yeung, Rob (2002) *The Ten Commandments: Equip Yourself with the 10 Most Important Skills to Move up the Career Ladder*. Oxford: How To Books Ltd

Index